Guilt-Free living

Arthur Meintjes

God's Word to the Nations. All rights reserved.

© 2015 by Arthur Meintjes

Published by Kingdom Life Ministry

Cover Design and Content Layout By: Catalyst Media

creatingcatalyst.com

Printed in the United States of America.

ISBN: 978-1519632654

CONTENTS

FOREWORD

The Bible is full of important Truth—but not every truth is created equal. The best way I can describe it is to say that the Bible contains truth from cover to cover, but not every truth contained in the Word is essential to our Christian walk. Not every truth is foundational to what we believe. It's what we believe about the essential (or foundational) truths of the New Testament that determines whether or not we experience the kind of guilt-free living God designed for us to live.

Many people know about God. They may even know about the Bible or have been influenced in some way by biblical thought, but most people have never experienced God for who He really is. Even those of us who desire to know God and read our Bibles daily, often misjudge what it says because we read it as a regular book from Genesis through to Revelation tending to think that it is a progressive revelation of God. But as New Testament believers, it is important to realize that there is only one true revelation of God, and that is Jesus Christ, His Son. John said:

> No man hath seen God at any time; the only begotten Son, which is in the bosom of the Father, he hath declared him.
>
> *John 1:18 (KJV)*

The Amplified version says:

> No man has ever seen God at any time; the only unique Son, or the only begotten God, Who is in the bosom [in the intimate presence] of the Father, He has declared Him [He has revealed Him and brought Him out where He can be seen; He has interpreted Him and He has made Him known].

According to this scripture, Jesus is the only One who has ever seen God for who He really is. He is the only One who fully represents who God is to us. Jesus Himself said, *"He that hath seen me hath seen the Father."* (John 14:9 KJV) That's why the writer of Hebrews said:

> The Son radiates God's own glory and expresses the very character of God, and he sustains everything by the mighty power of his command. When he had cleansed us from our sins, he sat down in the place of honor at the right hand of the majestic God in heaven.
>
> *Hebrews 1:3 (NLT)*

Jesus is the sole and exact representation of God. It is through Him and Him alone that we can correctly interpret what the Bible says about God and in turn, about us. Only through Jesus Christ and His finished work at Calvary, can we rightly understand the truths of

Scripture (both the Old and New Testament). He is the lens we must look through to know and experience God for who He really is.

Jesus (and His finished work) is *the* foundational and essential truth. He is the measure we must use to build and establish our beliefs and doctrines. *But what if I read something, Arthur, that doesn't line up with who Jesus is?* You cannot apply scripture outside the revelation of the Gospel. Any truth that does not fit within those constraints is not essential; it does not apply to us—even if it's in the Bible. *But Arthur, the Bible is true.* The Bible is true—but Jesus (who He is and what He accomplished in and through His finished work) is "the Truth!"

The Bible is God's history of dealings with mankind. Everything written in scripture is "God-breathed" according to 2 Timothy 3:16 (NIV). That means it is God-inspired. God inspired the men of the Bible to write down their experiences with Him in order to reveal Christ. Does that negate their experience? No. But does that mean their experience becomes Truth simply because it is in a book we call the Bible? No. We must learn to discern scripture just like we discern someone's personal testimony or experience today.

For example, a little old lady stands up in church to testify of God. She begins by praising God for getting her through another week of Satan's vicious attack. She thanks God for testing her patience like gold in the refiner's fire through her chronic sickness (old age). She blesses God for teaching her humility through her failure to read and pray like she should. And on she goes attributing things in her life to God that aren't part of His character. Does her belief system define who God is? No. God exists independently of our opinion of Him. Was her experience real to her? Of course. But does that "real" experience constitute truth? No! Unfortunately, her understanding of God can influence others' experiences if they do not have a personal relationship with the Truth.

This is exactly what happened in scripture. In the book of Job, we find a man of God experiencing tragedy, trials, and trouble. Throughout his trouble, friends come to "encourage him" with their interpretations and opinions of who God is and what Job needs to do to reconcile himself to God. Nine chapters of the book consist wholly of their opinions. These opinions were Spirit-inspired and recorded in scripture, but they were all wrong! At one point God even spoke to Job and said, *"Who is this that darkens counsel by words without knowledge?"* (Job 38:2 NKJV). And Job himself had to repent. Not for any wrong action he'd done that brought about his experience, but because he misinterpreted and misrepresented who God is. He said, *"Surely I spoke of things I did not understand…My ears had heard of you, but now my eyes have seen you…I repent."* (Job 41:3, 5-6 NIV) Job essentially said, "I let others tell me who You were but did not know You for myself."

We must be careful to know God for ourselves. We must learn to discern scripture, building upon the rock of Jesus Christ—the essential Truth—and not attempt to lay a foundation on the sandy shores of our limited knowledge or experience. Otherwise, we will never be able to experience the guilt-free life God designed for us in Him.

...But now you have had every stain washed off: now you have been set apart as holy: now you have been pronounced free from guilt; in the name of our Lord Jesus Christ and through the Spirit of our God.
1 Corinthians 6:11 (WNT)

Part One

THE UNFAIRNESS OF THE GOSPEL

If fairness is what you want—go to hell.

Chapter One

ESTABLISHING A NEW RELATIONSHIP WITH GOD

In the beginning, God desired relationship, and so He formed the heavens and the earth with that result in mind. He made Earth as a place for mankind to set his foot. God made the sun to warm man's face. He placed the moon, planets, and stars to mark the seasons and speak of His greatness. God created the animals and plants for man's food and enjoyment. He considered the elements and minerals necessary for man's creativity. He developed the water cycle, the oxygen cycle, the rock cycle, the seed, and the food chain to allow Earth to rejuvenate itself and provide for mankind indefinitely. Everything God made was created in preparation for His relationship with man.

But what kind of relationship was God after? Did He want robotic servants who would do whatever He said? Was God after groupies—people who would fall on their faces before Him and gush about how amazing He is? Did He desire dependent children to maintain His necessity? Or was He looking for friends and sons whom He could talk to and relate with? God wanted a family of sons and daughters—and that's what He created us to be.

Unfortunately, when Adam and Eve chose to sin, it changed their relationship with God. Even though God's idea of relationship and His good intention towards man did not change, Adam and Eve's did.

Now the serpent was more crafty than any of the wild animals the Lord God had made. He said to the woman, "Did God really say, 'You must not eat from any tree in the garden'?" ²The woman said to the serpent, "We may eat fruit from the trees in the garden, ³but God did say, 'You must not eat fruit from the tree that is in the middle of the garden, and you must not touch it, or you will die.'"⁴"You will not certainly die," the serpent said to the woman. ⁵"For God knows that when you eat from it your eyes will be opened, and you will be like God, knowing good and evil." ⁶When the woman saw that the fruit of the tree was good for food and pleasing to the eye, and also desirable for gaining wisdom, she took some and ate it. She also gave some to her husband, who was with her, and he ate it. ⁷Then the eyes of both of them were opened, and they realized they were naked; so they sewed fig leaves together and made coverings for themselves. ⁸Then the man and his wife heard the sound of the Lord God as he was walking in the garden in the cool of the day, and they hid from the Lord God among the trees of the garden. ⁹But the Lord God called to the man, "Where are you?" ¹⁰He answered, "I heard you in the garden, and I was

afraid because I was naked; so I hid."
Genesis 3:1-10 (NIV)

In Genesis 3, we see the serpent (the devil) entering history to tempt Adam and Eve. Up to this point, scripture indicates that God and man enjoyed an intimate, transparent relationship and open communication with each other—they were friends. But when the serpent came to tempt Adam and Eve, they began to question God's intentions toward them instead of remembering Him as their friend. They thought of the serpent's beguiling words. *Could God be holding out on me? Am I missing a benefit of this relationship?* And they decided to partake of the fruit of the Tree of Knowledge of Good and Evil to find out. Immediately, their "eyes opened, and they realized they were naked."

Now I believe this "nakedness" is referring to much more than physical nakedness. In Genesis 2:25, it says that Adam and Eve were naked and "felt no shame." They were not just physically naked, but their relationship with God and each other was intimate, open, and transparent. They had nothing to hide and nothing to fear. Shame did not exist. But when they chose to distrust and disobey God, those feelings of fear and shame immediately came to fill their minds and hearts.

But notice, God did not change. If we reread those verses, we will see that there is no indication that God was mad, upset, or disappointed. God still came to the Garden looking for Adam and Eve like He did regularly, every evening. God knew what happened, but His love, intentions, and purposes for mankind—His concept of relationship—did not change, even though Adam and Eve sinned. It was Adam and Eve's hearts, minds, and ideas of relationship that changed. Their feelings of shame kept them from experiencing the benefits of the intimate relationship and open and transparent friendship they had developed with God. So they ran to hide.

Covenant-Based Relationship

Mankind was never meant to live in guilt, shame, and fear. Those emotions are extremely debilitating. They limit what we can believe. They warp what we perceive. They create stress and force our bodies into "fight or flight mode." When our bodies are under stress, they are constantly trying to protect or guard themselves physically, emotionally, and mentally. Guilt, shame, and fear are detrimental to our relationships, our potential, our health, and our sanity. Doctors have researched the effects of emotional stress on the body and have determined that most of the deadly diseases known today are predominately stress-related. It's a big problem in our world (especially the western world). And it all started that day in the Garden. Since then, mankind has been dealing with these emotions and trying to find a new way of relating to God.

But how can we relate to a perfect and holy God? Some people believe they can cover their sin with good works so God will accept them. Others spend all their energy hiding their thoughts and attitudes by beating themselves into obedience. A few try to assuage their guilt by ignoring God's existence. Others create gods they can relate to—gods that are selfish, that lie, and react in anger. But no one can relate to God in these ways; no one can develop the type of friendship God desires based solely on their own efforts. No one can reach His standard. So God stepped in and reached out for relationship—an agreement between Himself and man through the man Abram.

In Genesis chapter seventeen, God introduced Himself to Abram and called him into relationship.

> *And when Abram was ninety years old and nine, the LORD appeared to Abram, and said unto him, I am the Almighty God; walk before me, and be thou perfect. ²And I will make my covenant between me and thee, and will multiply thee exceedingly.*
> *Genesis 17:1-2 (KJV)*

In the original Hebrew language, this verse is written a little differently. It essentially says, "I'm Almighty God. I'm coming to make covenant with you, but my standard (my requirement) is that you be perfect." Now Abram understood covenant relationship. When God came to him and said, "I am Almighty— the Creator of the universe, and I'm coming to make

Mankind was never meant to live in guilt, shame, and fear.

covenant with you," Abram probably thought, *YES!* He realized that being in covenant with God meant all his enemies would become God's enemies. He understood that no one could stand against him with God on his side. But then, God made it clear that Abram would have to meet His standard—perfection.

> *And Abram fell on his face ...*
> *Genesis 17:3a (KJV)*

I used to think Abram fell on his face out of reverence and worship—and maybe in a sense he did, but I believe he really fell on his face because he was overwhelmed. Abram had lived life; he was nearing one hundred years when God approached him. He knew what God was requiring was impossible. It's almost like somebody coming to you and offering you a million dollars if you can live the rest of your life without making another mistake. You'd know it was hopeless. I think Abram felt the same way. But again, God demonstrated, just like in the Garden, that His concept of relationship hadn't changed.

> *... and God talked with him, saying, ⁴As for me, behold, my covenant is with thee, and thou shalt be a father of many nations. ⁵Neither shall thy name any more be called Abram, but thy name shall be Abraham; for a father of many nations have I made thee. ⁶And I will make thee exceeding fruitful, and I will make nations of thee, and kings shall come out of thee. ⁷And I will establish my covenant between me and thee and thy seed after thee in their generations for an everlasting covenant, to be a God unto thee, and to thy seed after thee. ⁸And I will give unto thee, and to thy seed after thee, the land wherein thou art a stranger, all the land of Canaan, for an everlasting possession; and I will be their God.*
>
> *Genesis 17:3b-8 (KJV)*

When God spoke with Abram, He said, "Look Abram, this is what I'm going to do. You have nothing to fear; you have nothing to do with this, but **I'm** going to use you to establish my covenant of relationship with mankind. And by the way, I'm changing your name to Abraham so that you will always remember this day."

Not only did God change Abram's name, but He also had Abraham and his descendants circumcised.

Circumcision did nothing for God, but it was a poignant reminder to Abraham that He had a relationship. Circumcision became a sign of their agreement and a vivid picture of what covenant with God meant. Even though Abraham did not always live his life according to the standard of God's perfection, every time he saw the sign of the covenant, he remembered the promise of God's presence and blessing. A promised based on Who God is, not what he could do. Years later, Abraham's grandsons were still experiencing the blessing of the covenant because of whom they were related to.

Merit-Based Relationship

Fast-forward approximately 300 years as Moses led the people of Israel out of the land of Egypt. During their travels in the wilderness, God protected them and provided for them. He was with them and delivered them, not because of what they did but because they were the descendants of Abraham. God was showing the Israelites that He was in relationship with them.

Then the people came to Mt. Sinai. There they said to Moses, "You go up the mountain and find out what God wants from us." (Deut. 5:23-27) Instead of being content with an individual relationship with God, they desired something more—something external, something they could see and control. Maybe they felt the need to repay God for rescuing them. Maybe they thought His idea of relationship was too good to be true. Maybe they thought

God had ulterior motives for making the covenant with them. All we know is they weren't satisfied with a covenant based on genealogy. They wanted something based on what they could do for God.

So God spelled out His standard of perfection for them and gave it to the people. They called it the Law. It listed God's expectations of behavior, the consequences of disobedience, and the payment necessary for covering sin (their lawbreaking) so He could freely work on their behalf to bring peace, prosperity, healing, and safety to them.

God chose the Israelites to be His friends and demonstrate His goodness in the earth. But they struggled to uphold the standard the law required and often forgot about their relationship with God. However, every time they faced adversity, the Israelites would remember their agreement and seek out the benefits of their relationship once more. In the Old Testament, we often see them offering sacrifices that would cover their sin and allow God to work on their behalf. One of those occasions is found in First Samuel chapter seven.

> *When the Philistine rulers heard that Israel had gathered at Mizpah, they mobilized their army and advanced. The Israelites were badly frightened when they learned that the Philistines were approaching. [8]"Don't stop pleading with the Lord our God to save us from the Philistines!" they begged Samuel. [9]So Samuel took a young lamb and offered it to the Lord as a whole burnt offering. He pleaded with the Lord to help Israel, and the Lord answered him. 1 Samuel 7:7-9 (NLT)*

During this time in history, the Philistine army was

greatly feared throughout the Middle East. They had a reputation as a well-trained war machine. They were brutal in battle. They gloried in taking captives and torturing them. And they ruthlessly killed women, children, and old men. Sometimes, when they entered new territory, the rulers of the land would simply surrender rather than face the Philistine's horrifying reputation. (How many times do we do that? How often do we surrender to the reputations of disease or financial crisis even before encountering their symptoms? Have we forgotten that *reputation* just means *"something **believed** about a person or a thing?")*

When the Philistines appeared in Israel, the Bible says the people were "badly frightened." I imagine the men were picturing themselves being tortured. They probably saw their daughters and wives raped and their sons shackled and taken to the slave market. But in the midst of their fear, the Israelites remembered their Friend and asked Samuel to sacrifice to the Lord and plead for His help. They understood that if they turned to the Lord and offered a burnt sacrifice to cover their sin, God could work on their behalf.

"Don't stop pleading with the Lord our God," they begged Samuel. So Samuel took a young lamb and offered it to the Lord as a burnt offering. Now this lamb was not just any lamb. In order to offer it to God, it had to be a special lamb. To find the perfect lamb in those days, priests (who carried the instructions for offerings) would go into a flock and start looking for a lamb without spot, blemish, or defect. Every lamb that looked pure would be thoroughly examined. They would look at its coat, feel its legs, and check its belly and mouth. They would inspect every inch of the lamb, and when they found one that met the requirements prescribed by law, the priests would hoist it in the air and shout "the Lamb of God!" The people who heard would begin rejoicing and follow the priests repeating, "the Lamb of God!" Soon a crowd would gather to dance and sing songs about the lamb. They understood their deliverance and victory was in the lamb!

> When the lamb was offered, it became their doorway to relationship.

The Israelites knew that when Samuel offered sacrifice to the Lord that day, their sins would be covered. They understood that when they stood before the Lord sinless, God could work on their behalf. Their victory would cease to be about their strength or wisdom; it wouldn't depend on their abilities at all. When the lamb was offered, it became their doorway to relationship. Notice what happened in verse ten:

> *Just as Samuel was sacrificing the burnt offering, the Philistines arrived to attack Israel. But the Lord spoke with a mighty voice of thunder from heaven that day, and the Philistines were thrown into such confusion that the Israelites defeated them. [11] The men of Israel chased them from Mizpah to a place below Beth-car, slaughtering them all along the way…[13a] So the Philistines were subdued and didn't invade Israel again for some time.*
>
> *1 Samuel 7:10-11, 13a (NLT)*

The Israelites didn't just win the battle. God disarmed the armies of Philistia, and "the men of Israel chased them, slaughtering them along the way!" When Israel remembered their relationship with the Lord and offered sacrifice to cover their sin, all they had to do was fight their enemy's backside! God did the rest. For that moment, they gloried in the benefits of relationship with God. The only problem was their sacrifices could not remove sin or the feelings of condemnation and guilt from their hearts. Inevitably, the people would fall back into the habits and patterns of thinking that kept God from working on their behalf to begin with. Their sacrifices only covered their sin for a moment.

Grace-Based Relationship

The old system under the law of Moses was only a shadow, a dim preview of the good things to come, not the good things themselves. The sacrifices under that system were repeated again and again, year after year, but they were never able to provide perfect cleansing for those who came to worship. ²If they could have provided perfect cleansing, the sacrifices would have stopped, for the worshipers would have been purified once for all time, and their feelings of guilt would have disappeared...⁴For it is not possible for the blood of bulls and goats to take away sins.
Hebrews 10:1-2, 4 (NLT)

Mankind needed a different type of agreement with God. We needed something that could be applied to all people, not just the Israelites. And we needed something that wasn't based on our ability. Like Paul said, we aspired to do what was good and experience the benefits of relationship with God, but no matter how hard we tried, we couldn't seem to carry out the good we desired (Rom.

7:15-23). Because *"the law is holy, and the commandment is holy, righteous and good…but [we are] unspiritual, sold as a slave to sin."* (Rom. 7:12, 14)

> *I have the desire to do what is good, but I cannot carry it out…²⁴What a wretched man I am! Who will rescue me from this body that is subject to death? ²⁵Thanks be to God, who delivers me through Jesus Christ our Lord!*
>
> Romans 7:18b, 24-25a (NIV)

The law was perfectly holy (Ps. 19:7), but man's involvement in that covenant was defective. Hebrews says, "If that first covenant had been without defect, there would have been no room for another one or an attempt to institute another one." (Hebrews 8:7) So God established a new contract (covenant)—a new agreement—through the finished work of the man, Christ Jesus!

> *For God so greatly loved and dearly prized the world that He [even] gave up His only begotten (unique) Son, so that whoever believes in (trusts in, clings to, relies on) Him shall not perish (come to destruction, be lost) but have eternal (everlasting) life.17For God did not send the Son into the world in order to judge (to reject, to condemn, to pass sentence on) the world, but that the world might find salvation and be made safe and sound through Him.*
>
> John 3:16-17

> *"Don't misunderstand why I have come. I did not come to abolish the law of Moses or the writings of the prophets. No, I came to accomplish their purpose.*
>
> Matthew 5:17 (NLT)

Chapter Two

GOD'S RISK: THE GOSPEL OF GRACE

Jesus came to fulfill every legal requirement of the law and satisfy its demands. He came to be our "Lamb of God!" At Christ's birth, God announced His good intentions toward us by sending angels to sing, "Glory to God in the highest, and on earth peace, good will toward men." (Luke 2:14 KJV) God still wanted relationship with us. He still desired the type of relationship and friendship He had with man in the Garden. His intentions, plans, and purposes toward man never changed, but neither did His standard (1 Sam. 15:29).

Though the law rightly communicated God's standard for relationship (perfection), it could do nothing about the heart issue of sin mankind struggled with. The law only exposed our sin; it made sin apparent and highlighted the great divide between God's standard and our capabilities. Though the law was good, the only thing it produced in its hearers was guilt and condemnation (Rom. 3:19-20). But when Jesus came, everything changed!

> *But when the set time had fully come, God sent his Son, born of a woman, born under the law, ⁵to redeem those under the law, that we might receive adoption to sonship.*
>
> *Galatians 4:4-5 (NIV)*

> *The law of Moses was unable to save us because of the weakness of our sinful nature. So God did what the law could not do. He sent his own Son in a body like the bodies we sinners have. And in that body God declared an end to sin's control over us by giving his Son as a sacrifice for our sins.*
>
> *Romans 8:3 (NLT)*

Our Lamb of God

In the gospel of John, Jesus approached His cousin, John the Baptist, to be baptized. John was a man who came to Israel preaching repentance. His mission was to prepare the people of God to receive the Perfect Lamb who would not just cover their sin but permanently remove it.

When Jesus came to be baptized, the Bible says John saw Him and shouted, *"the Lamb of God, who takes away the sin of the world!"* (John 1:29) As Gentiles, we might miss this inference, but remember John was speaking to Jews—to Israelites. These people understood the phrase "the lamb of God"; they heard it all the time (although never in reference to a man). They knew what benefits offering a sacrificial lamb would have. They knew that the "Lamb of God" meant their deliverance, salvation, and provision was at hand. John even qualified this Lamb's work by saying, *"the Lamb of God who takes away the sin of the world."* When the people heard John's declaration and saw Jesus, they turned to look at the man who would provide for each of their needs and restore them to an intimate relationship with God that wasn't based on their ability or performance.

> ## Jesus' sacrifice accomplished something far greater than any Old Covenant sacrifice.

Jesus' sacrifice accomplished something far greater than any Old Covenant sacrifice. His atonement was not just for a fleeting moment so God could act on our behalf. Jesus' life and death fulfilled the requirements of the law. It eliminated the heart issue of sin and the consequences of guilt and condemnation mankind had faced since the Garden of Eden. Hebrews says Jesus' sacrifice took care of sin and opened up relationship with God "once for all!"

> *For God's will was for us to be made holy by the sacrifice of the body of Jesus Christ, once for all time. [11]Under the old covenant, the priest stands and ministers before the altar day after day, offering the same sacrifices again and again, which can never take away sins. [12]But our High Priest offered himself to God as a single sacrifice for sins, good for all time. Then he sat down in the place of honor at God's right hand…[16]"This is the new covenant I will make with my people on that day, says the Lord: I will put my laws in their hearts, and I will write them on their*

minds." ¹⁷Then he says, "I will never again remember their sins and lawless deeds." ¹⁸And when sins have been forgiven, there is no need to offer any more sacrifices.

Hebrews 10:10-12, 16-18 (NLT)

There is now no more need of sacrifice. Jesus' sacrifice accomplished far more than any Old Testament priest! Did you know that there were no chairs or couches or anywhere to sit in the tabernacle or temple? The old covenant priest's job was never finished; he couldn't sit down. He had to offer sacrifices continually. But Jesus settled the issue of sin that was between God and man; it has been eliminated for all time, all people, and all sin. In the original language of Hebrews chapter ten, the word used for sin is not a plural verb (meaning a lot of bad things you do). It is a singular noun (meaning the whole issue of sin). Jesus didn't just cover our sin and hide it from God's view like in the Old Testament atonement. He completely exchanged His life for ours and fulfilled the law on our behalf to not only eliminate sin as an issue between God and man, but also the guilt and condemnation that accompanied it. (All we have to do is believe.)

So what does that mean? Has God's standard changed? Is the law no longer in affect? No. God's standard has not and will never change, but since Jesus upheld the standard of perfection in our place, He fulfilled the law. And with the fulfillment of the law came the removal of the consequences of our failure, including guilt, fear, condemnation, and shame.

Having cancelled and blotted out and wiped away the handwriting of the note (bond) with its legal decrees and demands which was in force and stood against us (hostile to us). This [note with its regulations, decrees, and demands] He set aside and cleared completely out of our way by nailing it to [His] cross.

Colossians 2:14

Surely He has borne our griefs (sicknesses, weaknesses, and distresses) and carried our sorrows and pains [of punishment], yet we [ignorantly] considered Him stricken, smitten, and afflicted by God [as if with leprosy]. ⁵But He was wounded for our transgressions, He was bruised for our guilt and iniquities; the chastisement [needful to obtain] peace and well-being for us was upon Him, and with the stripes [that wounded] Him we are healed and made whole. ⁶All we like sheep have gone astray, we have turned every one to his own way; and the Lord has made to light upon Him the guilt and iniquity of us all.

Isaiah 53:4-6

Our relationship with God is no longer based on what we do or how well we keep the Ten Commandments. It is based on what Jesus did! Our acceptance, righteousness, and justification is no longer dependent on our performance. Neither is our participation in and experience of relationship with God dependent on our sanctification or holiness. How? By Grace through faith.

For it is by free grace (God's unmerited favor) that you are saved (delivered from judgment and made partakers of Christ's salvation) through [your] faith. And this [salvation] is not of yourselves [of your own doing, it came not through your own striving], but it is the gift of God; Not because of works [not the fulfillment of the Law's demands], lest any man should boast. [It is not the result of what anyone can

19

possibly do, so no one can pride himself in it or take glory to himself.]

Ephesians 2:8-9

For God's gifts and His call are irrevocable. [He never withdraws them when once they are given, and He does not change His mind about those to whom He gives His grace or to whom He sends His call.]

Romans 11:29

People always ask, "But doesn't grace give people a license to sin?" To which I must respond, "No. Grace simply exposes the motivations of our hearts." The Grace of God is what leads people to repentance (Rom. 2:4). It is the unearned, undeserved, irrevocable goodness of God. So where does that leave good behavior and responsibility? Right where it belongs—as a heart issue. Someone once told me, "This message is too risky to preach. There's no telling what people will do if they get that free!" But the truth is, it is God who took a risk with Grace. He decided He was tired of lip service—He wanted real relationship again!

> # When we realize we can live by grace, we stop pretending to be good for the sake of avoiding hell.

The Lord says: "These people come near to me with their mouth and honor me with their lips, but their hearts are far from me. Their worship of me is based on merely human rules they have been taught. ^{14}Therefore once more I will astound these people with wonder upon wonder; the wisdom of the wise will perish, the intelligence of the intelligent

will vanish." ¹⁵*Woe to those who go to great depths to hide their plans from the Lord, who do their work in darkness and think, "Who sees us? Who will know?"*
Isaiah 29:13-15 (NIV)

Heart Change

Grace exposes the motivations of our hearts. When we realize we can live by grace, we stop pretending to be good for the sake of avoiding hell. We stop serving God outwardly. Before God's Grace was given in Christ, we couldn't do right or live with right motives. It wasn't a part of our nature. Even the Pharisees, the religious leaders of Jesus' day, failed at it. And they were so zealous for righteousness that they not only taught the people to obey the Law of Moses but added extraneous practices to it to ensure no commandments were violated. For example, when the law said to wash your hands before eating, the Pharisees told the people to wash their hands, wrists, and forearms to the elbow. And when the law said, "Honor the Sabbath by doing no regular work," the Pharisees said, "do not walk more than half a mile in a straight line outside your city walls." (Hecht, 2015) Sometimes the Pharisees even added to the law to allow them to bend its original intent. For example, when the law said, "Honor your father and mother," the Pharisees said, "if we give our excess to God then we are released from honoring our parents by providing for them in their old age." (Mark 7:9-13) But according to Jesus, their obedience to the "letter of the law" missed the "spirit of the law".

What sorrow awaits you teachers of religious law and you Pharisees. Hypocrites! For you are careful to tithe even the tiniest income from your herb gardens, but you ignore the more important aspects of the law—justice, mercy, and faith. You should tithe, yes, but do not neglect the more important things. ²⁴Blind guides! You strain your water so you won't accidentally swallow a gnat, but you swallow a camel!

Matthew 23:23-24 (NLT)

In His famous Sermon on the Mount, Jesus talked about this issue in depth. Throughout the entire monologue, He spoke of the heart issues the law couldn't change. He spoke not only of righteousness but of perfection. He said things like, "The Law says, 'Do not murder,' but I tell you do not hate your brother or speak ill of him." And "The Law says, 'Do not commit adultery,' but I tell you if you have looked at a woman lustfully you have already broken the commandment." Jesus even went as far as to say, "The Law says, 'Love your neighbor,' but I say love your enemies. If you only love those who love you how are you different from the Gentiles? Be perfect as your heavenly Father is perfect." (Matt. 5:21-48)

Unfortunately, the church has not understood what Jesus was saying. They've missed His point as much as the Pharisees did. They say, "Jesus told us to obey the law. It's in red, so we've got to at least do that!" But let's be honest. If Jesus was telling us to obey the law and live life in perfection in order to have relationship with God, we might as well quit now. There is no hope. Just close that Bible—in fact, throw it away—and go live your life. If we have to relate to God based on our own goodness, we'd be doomed. Even if we managed to control what our bodies do (like not killing someone or committing adultery with our neighbor), how could we change our heart attitudes? We couldn't—it's impossible.

And that's what Jesus was saying in the Sermon on the Mount. He was speaking to a bunch of people born under the law, born trying to reach God's standard in their own strength. Up to this point, there was no other way to relate to God. At this point in history, Jesus hadn't died in our place. He couldn't tell the people about Grace. He couldn't tell them not to worry about the law. When He was speaking to the people, the law was still in full force. It hadn't been fulfilled allowing us to relate to God outside of it. That's why Jesus said, "Whosoever therefore shall break one of these least commandments and shall teach men so, he shall be called the least in the kingdom of heaven." (Matt. 5:19 KJV)

When Jesus spoke to the people, He was essentially saying, "Don't you see? Keeping the law is impossible for you. You can't reach God's standard of holiness. Even the Pharisees, though they spend all their time spelling out physical holiness, can't meet God's standard of **heart** perfection."

Except your righteousness shall exceed the righteousness of the scribes and Pharisees, ye shall in no case enter into the kingdom of heaven.
Mathew 5:20 (KJV)

Unless you do far better than the Pharisees in the matters of right living, you won't know the first thing about entering the kingdom. (MSG)

The sacrifices of the Old Testament couldn't reach into our hearts and change our natures. Only God could do that. That's why we needed Grace; that's why we need a Savior who would exchange His life for ours. According to Merriam-Webster, grace is "divine assistance; special favor; and privilege given because of one's heritage" (Merriam-Webster, 1993). Grace is way more than just God's attitude towards us; it is His ability in us that enables us to step into the freedom of the finished work of Jesus Christ. It is His ability to live without guilt, fear, or shame.

I'll give you a new heart, put a new spirit in you. I'll remove the stone heart from your body and replace it with a heart that's God-willed, not self-willed. ²⁷I'll put my Spirit in you and make it possible for you to do what I tell you and live by my commands.
Ezekiel 36:26-27 (MSG)

This is an illustration for the present time, indicating that the gifts and sacrifices being offered were not able to clear the conscience of the worshiper. ¹⁰They are only a matter of food and drink and various ceremonial washings--external regulations applying until the time of the new order. ¹¹But when Christ came as high priest of the good things that are now already here, he went through the greater and more perfect tabernacle that is not made with human hands, that is to say, is not a part of this creation. ¹²He did not enter by means of the blood of goats and calves; but he entered the Most Holy Place once for all by his own blood, thus obtaining eternal redemption. ¹³For if the blood of goats and bulls and the ashes of a heifer sprinkled on those who are ceremonially unclean sanctify them so that they are outwardly clean. ¹⁴How much more, then, will the blood of Christ, who through the

eternal Spirit offered himself unblemished to God, cleanse our consciences from acts that lead to death, so that we may serve the living God!
Hebrews 9:9-14 (NIV)

Just like God first developed relationship with Abraham by grace and continued relationship with Abraham's children because of whom they were related to, God has chosen to deal with us by grace, and when we realize that we are related to Christ through His finished work, we choose to believe!

...it is His ability in us that enables us to step into the freedom of the finished work of Jesus Christ.

I am crucified with Christ: nevertheless I live; yet not I, but Christ liveth in me: and the life which I now live in the flesh I live by the faith of the Son of God, who loved me, and gave himself for me.
Galatians 2:20 (KJV)

We are made right with God by placing our faith in Jesus Christ. And this is true for everyone who believes, no matter who we are.
Romans 3:22 (NLT)

Because you are his sons, God sent the Spirit of his Son into our hearts, the Spirit who calls out, "Abba, Father." 7So you are no longer a slave, but God's child; and since you are his child, God has made you also an heir.
Galatians 4:6-7 (NIV)

This resurrection life you received from God is not a timid, grave-tending life. It's adventurously expectant, greeting God with a childlike "What's next, Papa?" God's Spirit touches our spirits and confirms who we really are. We know who he is, and we know who we are: Father and children. And we know we are going to get what's coming to us—an unbelievable inheritance!

Romans 8:15-17 (MSG)

When God does relationship, He does it right!

Part Two

BETWEEN TWO
COVENANTS

God is satisfied…when will you be satisfied?

Chapter Three

MESSAGE OF RECONCILIATION

There is no force more destructive in the life of a believer than that of a guilty conscience. Yet the majority of Christians around the world believe that being weighed down and crippled with condemnation and guilt is part of the normal Christian experience. We've become so used to the feelings of guilt, shame, and condemnation that we don't even notice them anymore. And worse, we think those feelings somehow improve our Christian walk.

Many believers don't know how to function without a guilty conscience. They don't know how to relate to God outside of their feelings of shame, condemnation, and guilt. It's sad, but most Christians believe a measure of guilt is beneficial to their lives. They feel it serves a worthy purpose by keeping them motivated to do good works and live holy. But that's not the type of relationship

God designed us for.

I don't feel guilty, you say. *I'm just a little leery* (or respectful or circumspect) *of my relationship with God.* You can call it whatever you want, but if you believe you have to perform to a certain standard or fulfill some duty in order to approach God, you've missed the real message of the cross. You've taken a "form of godliness but denied its power" like Second Timothy 3:5 says. You're living between two covenants, mixing a little of the New with the Old.

I know; I struggled with that. For nearly half my Christian life, I believed the only way I could really please God like Jesus did was to feel so guilty that I would be forced into doing His will. The only reason I had a prayer life or read my Bible in those days was because I felt guilty when I didn't; and I was a pastor! (Of course, I would never have said it out loud—but I hated getting up at five o'clock in the morning to read my Bible and pray. Now if you can do that—and enjoy it—more power to you. But I couldn't. I only did those things because I'd heard that's what good Christians did and how good Christians experienced the favor of God or His anointing.)

I'm sure I was limited in what I received from God because of that attitude, but it wasn't always like that. When I first became a believer, no one had to tell me to read my Bible. I wanted to read it. I couldn't put it down. Everywhere I went I had my Bible. Even going into a restaurant for a quick bite to eat, my Bible would be with me at the table. Then I went to church and discovered that Bible reading was a "requirement" to victorious Christian living. All of a sudden, I began having to force myself to read the Bible. I even took one popular preacher's advice and read my Bible in the shower so that if I fell asleep, I would hit the hard floor and wake up to finish my required hour. (I only managed that a couple of times before the balls of my feet hurt too bad to stand!) I was discovering first-hand what Romans was talking about when it said:

> *Therefore by the deeds of the law there shall no flesh be justified in his sight: for by the law is the knowledge of sin.*
>
> *Romans 3:20 (KJV)*

Instead of living in the freedom that Christ bought for me and allowing that freedom to produce right motives, I began doing those things out of a guilty conscience. I thought, *If I can just discipline myself to read more chapters and pray longer, I know God would be pleased with me. I know I'd experience His victory.* It wasn't that the things I was trying to do weren't good or important, but my motive for doing them was wrong. (By the way, the only difference between good works and dead works is motive. That means if we only pray out of obligation, even our prayer life can be a dead work.)

Living with a Guilty Conscience

We've all experienced times when we've been motivated partially or wholly by guilt. As a matter of fact, guilt has been a limiting hindrance in our relationship with God ever since the Garden of Eden. Guilt limits us when we read the Bible; it hinders us from seeing the Truth written within it. (That's why there are so many denominations, groupings, and sects within the Body of Christ.) Guilt limits us when we pray. It hinders us from hearing God's still, small voice. Guilt limits us when we stand in faith. It causes us to doubt God's goodness or our worthiness and hinders us from receiving from God. Guilt is NOT a Christian emotion!

Guilt is defined as *"the feeling of responsibility or remorse for an offense, crime, or wrong committed whether it be real or imagined."* (Dictionary.com) A healthy conscience (the kind all believers should have) recognizes when its behavior has been hurtful to others, destructive to itself, or unacceptable in society. This type of conscience regulates our interactions with others and keeps us

Jesus came to free us from the control of sin, but also the guilt that accompanied it.

from becoming psychopaths. The opposite of this, and the place many Christians live, is in the destructive realm of a guilty conscience. A guilty conscience believes it has offended a holy and righteous God and therefore stands condemned, separated, and excluded from relationship with Him. Destructive guilt says, "I'm unacceptable before God and deserving of His judgment and punishment." It might not say, *God is going to kill me,* but it always says, *I'm not worthy; God isn't obligated to honor His promise to me. I've disqualified myself.*

Jesus came to free us from the control of sin, but also the guilt that accompanied it. Our everyday lives should not be consumed with thinking about sin. Neither should regret for all the stupid things we've done fill our days and nights.

> *How much more surely shall the blood of Christ, Who by virtue of [His] eternal Spirit [His own preexistent divine personality] has offered Himself as an unblemished sacrifice to God, purify our consciences from dead works and lifeless observances to serve the [ever] living God?*
>
> *Hebrews 9:14*

> *Surely He has borne our griefs (sicknesses, weaknesses, and distresses) and carried our sorrows and pains [of punishment], yet we [ignorantly] considered Him stricken, smitten, and afflicted by God [as if with leprosy]. ⁵But He was wounded for our transgressions, He was bruised for our guilt and iniquities; the chastisement [needful to obtain] peace and well-being for us was upon Him, and with the stripes [that wounded] Him we are healed and made whole.*
>
> *Isaiah 53:4-5*

> *The Law has merely a rude outline (foreshadowing) of the good things to come—instead of fully expressing those things—it can never by offering the same sacrifices continually year after year make perfect those who approach [its altars].²For if it were otherwise, would [these sacrifices] not have stopped being offered? Since the worshipers had once for all been cleansed, they would no longer have any guilt or consciousness of sin.*
>
> *Hebrews 10:1-2*

Hebrews says, because of Jesus' work, we should no longer have even the "consciousness of sin." Consciousness means "knowing" or "being aware of." (Dictionary.com)

So obviously, Hebrews is not saying it's okay to become a psychopath—that would be in opposition to the rest of scripture. We can't go around hurting others, destroying property, and doing whatever else pops into our brains without conviction or remorse—that would make us psychopaths and personify the complete opposite of Christlikeness. What we must do is learn to discern the difference between a healthy conscience towards others and the destructive emotions of condemnation and guilt towards God. This verse in Hebrews is saying we should no longer be aware of our sin or continue holding on to the perception of guilt. It is referring to our relationship with God. That relationship should exude freedom, not guilt or consciousness of sin.

> *The Messiah has set us free so that we may enjoy the benefits of freedom...*
>
> *Galatians 5:1 (ISV)*

Jesus—Our Lightening Rod

Jesus gave us freedom—not just freedom from sin but freedom from guilt, shame, and condemnation. We no longer need to be concerned with judgment. We do not need to be afraid that God will discover our sin. Sin is not on God's mind!

When Christ came, the angel told Mary to *"call him Jesus for he will save his people from their sin."* (Matt. 1:21) Another translation says Jesus came to *"deliver his people from the consequences of their sin."* (Ps. 130:8 NET) Think about a lightning rod. When people put lightning rods on houses or other buildings, its purpose is protection.

They anchor that rod into the ground so that if lightning strikes during a storm, it will hit the lightning rod and be deflected into the ground. Jesus came to this earth as a lightning rod. He became the instrument of God's justice against sin. Through His own body, God dealt with the issue of sin, once and for all, so that you and I could be saved from destruction and the consequence of our sin (John 9:39, 12:27).

Jesus said, in John 12:32, *"And I, if I be lifted up from the earth, will draw all **men** unto me."* (KJV) In the King James Version, the word "men" is italicized. That means it wasn't in the original text; it was added for clarity or to better fit our rules of grammar. So Jesus never said that word. That means the original text translates as, "I be lifted up will draw all unto me." That doesn't seem to make a lot of sense unless we look at the context. In the verse right before this, Jesus is talking about judgment and says, "Now is the judgment of this world..." (John 12:31). And later John adds, "This he said, signifying what death he should die." (John 12:33) I think that is significant. Jesus, talking about judgment, says He will "draw all" to Himself, and John says, "He's talking about His own death." So this verse could actually be translated, "When I die on the cross, I will draw all of God's judgment against sin to myself. I will become the lightning rod so that no human being will ever have to suffer judgment and the consequences of God's justice against sin!"

> *For God so greatly loved and dearly prized the world that He [even] gave up His only begotten (unique) Son, so that whoever believes in (trusts in, clings to, relies on) Him shall not perish (come to destruction, be lost) but have eternal (everlasting) life. [17]For*

God did not send the Son into the world in order to judge (to reject, to condemn, to pass sentence on) the world, but that the world might find salvation and be made safe and sound through Him. [18]He who believes in Him [who clings to, trusts in, relies on Him] is not judged [he who trusts in Him never comes up for judgment; for him there is no rejection, no condemnation—he incurs no damnation]; but he who does not believe (cleave to, rely on, trust in Him) is judged already [he has already been convicted and has already received his sentence] because he has not believed in and trusted in the name of the only begotten Son of God.[He is condemned for refusing to let his trust rest in Christ's name.]

John 3:16-18

God's Choice

Jesus suffered for us! His sacrifice on the cross was different than any old covenant sacrifices. His blood didn't just cover our sin. It didn't hide our sin. Jesus' sacrifice removed our sin! He went to court for all mankind and once, for all time, dealt with the penalty for our sin. The case against humanity has been dismissed, and we are free! But *I don't deserve that,* you say. It doesn't matter. God made a choice. It was Him we'd sinned against, and it was His right to decide how to deal with our sin. And God **chose** mercy and grace. He **chose** reconciliation. He **chose** relationship.

Therefore, when Christ came into the world, he said: "Sacrifice and offering you did not desire, but a body you prepared for me; [6]with burnt offerings and sin offerings you were not pleased. [7]Then I said, 'Here

*I am—it is written about me in the scroll—I have
come to do your will, my God.'"...¹⁰And by that will,
we have been made holy through the sacrifice of the
body of Jesus Christ once for all...¹⁴For by one sacrifice
he has made perfect forever those who are being made
holy. ¹⁵The Holy Spirit also testifies to us about this.
First, he says, ¹⁶"This is the covenant I will make
with them after that time, says the Lord. I will put
my laws in their hearts, and I will write them on
their minds." ¹⁷Then he adds: "Their sins and lawless
acts I will remember no more."*
Hebrews 10:5-7, 10, 14-17 (NIV) [emphasis added]

*Still, it's what God had in mind all along, to crush
him with pain. The plan was that he give himself as
an offering for sin so that he'd see life come from it—
life, life, and more life. And God's plan will deeply
prosper through him.*
Isaiah 53:10 (MSG)

*But how can God "be okay" with my sin? How can He
forget the ugliness of it?* Did you miss the part of Hebrews
ten that says, "Their sins and lawless acts I will remember
no more"? It didn't say, "Their sin and lawbreaking, I will
forget." It said God wouldn't remember our sin. There's
a difference between forgetting and not remembering.
Forgetting means, "I want to remember—I'm trying to
remember—but I can't." Not remembering is different.
Not remembering is a choice. It says, "I could remember
if I wanted to, but I choose not to remember." And that's
what God did with our sin.

*Now where there is **absolute** remission (forgiveness and cancellation of the penalty) of these [sins and lawbreaking], there is no longer any offering made to atone for sin.*

Hebrews 10:18 (emphasis added)

Our sin is not dancing around the fringes of God's mind. He's not looking for it. He has chosen not to remember! So every time you come to God and say, "Oh God, I'm such a horrible child—I'm a sinner. I can't seem to stop sinning." He says, "I don't know what you're talking about. The issue of sin between you and Me has been dealt with. I am satisfied."

Praise God, sin is not on God's mind! So what is? Reconciliation. Second Corinthians says:

This means that anyone who belongs to Christ has become a new person. The old life is gone; a new life has begun! ¹⁸And all of this is a gift from God, who brought us back to himself through Christ. And God has given us this task of reconciling people to him. ¹⁹For God was in Christ, reconciling the world to himself, no longer counting people's sins against them. And he gave us this wonderful message of reconciliation.

2 Corinthians 5:17-19 (NLT)

In other words, God was using Christ to restore his relationship with humanity. He didn't hold people's faults against them, and he has given us this message of restored relationships to tell others.

(GW)

The moment you understand what Christ has done, everything changes. Your opinion of God changes, but your opinion of yourself and others changes as well. You realize God didn't turn His back on you; He always loved you and thought so much of you that He gave up His own Son to have intimate relationship with you. Years ago, I was in a McDonald's picking up a quick lunch. It was a typical McDonald's, full of ordinary, working people. I was wearing a black t-shirt I'd had made that said, *Did you know...* real big on the front. When I walked into McDonald's and got in line, I noticed a man looking at me. He was a big man with long, dirty hair and dirty jeans. He had on a tool belt and muddy boots and was obviously a construction worker on his lunch break. Anyway, he jumped in line behind me, and I swear I could feel his eyes reading the back of my shirt. It said, *Did you know... God is not holding your sin against you?* and included the verse from 2 Corinthians 5:19. Soon I heard, "*!&$*^@! Why has nobody told me that?!" And I turned to see that big man's eyes welling up with tears. "Is that true?" he asked.

The moment you understand what Christ has done, everything changes.

"Yes, it is," I responded.

"What do I need to do?" he said.

"Believe," I told him. "The Bible says, 'believe in the Lord Jesus Christ, and you will be saved.'" And I simply walked him to Christ as Paul admonished us, *"Therefore, we are ambassadors for Christ, as though God were making an appeal through us; we beg you on behalf of Christ, be reconciled to God."* (2 Cor. 5:20 NASB)

The JB Phillips Translation puts this beautifully. *"We are now Christ's ambassadors, as though God were appealing direct to you through us. As his personal representatives we say, "Make your peace with God."* (2 Cor. 5:20 JBP)

God has called the entire world to Himself. At the cross, He removed all obstacles to relationship with Him, and shouted, "I am satisfied!" Now the ball is in our court. When will we be satisfied with what Jesus accomplished? When will we decide to believe and be reconciled to Him?

Chapter Four

FALLEN FROM GRACE

Have you ever felt like you didn't measure up to God's standard? Most Christians feel this way. In fact, many feel they need to obtain a certain level of holiness before God can help them or even hear their prayers. But Colossians says that Christ has presented us to God holy, blameless, and above reproach (Col. 1:22). Hebrews tells us we can now come before God "boldly." (Heb. 4:16) But if we truly believed this, the nagging fears of imperfection and unworthiness wouldn't continually hinder us from receiving from God or approaching Him.

Believers often do not realize that the reason they're experiencing the feelings of guilt and condemnation is because they have allowed a toxic mixture of Old Testament law and New Testament hope to infiltrate their belief system. As a matter of fact, the amount of guilt and condemnation we experience as believers is directly proportional to the mixture of performance and grace we live with each day. Remember, "a little leaven leavens the whole lump!" (Gal.5:9)

He exchanged His life, His righteousness, for ours and made us holy.

The idea that we need to become more holy—or that we even can—is the biggest lie of legalistic, religious Christianity. If what Jesus accomplished on the cross wasn't enough to remove our sin and put us in right relationship with God, what do we think our feeble, selfish actions can accomplish? We can't do anything to make ourselves holy or righteous, but Hebrews tells us that Jesus did. He exchanged His life, His righteousness, for ours and made us holy.

> *And by that will, we have been made holy through the sacrifice of the body of Jesus Christ once for all.*
>
> *Hebrews 10:10 (NIV)*

> *...But now you have had every stain washed off: now you have been set apart as holy: now you have been pronounced free from guilt; in the name of our Lord Jesus Christ and through the Spirit of our God.*
> *1 Corinthians 6:11 (WNT)*

> *For by one offering he hath perfected for ever them that are sanctified.*
> *Hebrews 10:14 (KJV)*

The problem is, we haven't learned to see things from God's perspective. We've alienated ourselves from His life by living between two covenants (Col.1:21).

When things are going well, and we feel we've lived up to God's standard, it's easy for us to trust in what Christ accomplished. It's easy for us to lean on grace and shout "Amen" in church services. It's easy to commune with God, to know that He hears us, and will work on our behalf. It's easy to have faith. But when we haven't lived up to God's standard, when we feel condemned, we find ourselves gravitating towards the rules and regulations of the law to try and bring ourselves back into "holiness."

But living between two covenants was NOT the kind of life God intended for His children. That kind of living is like attempting to survive a losing battle in enemy territory. We didn't make ourselves holy, and we certainly can't make ourselves more holy! No matter how hard we try, our work only perpetuates the feelings of guilt and condemnation we try to avoid. It leaches the strength and joy from our relationship with God.

Squandering Grace

It is easy to fall into the trap of rule-based performance (though I know that is not what most Christians intend when they begin following rules); we all want to do the "right thing." The law appeals to the finite part of our brains that looks for order, pattern, and rules amidst the chaos of life. Our brains shout, Yes! *This is good*, when we hear suggestions to fast and pray "and watch God move." We think, *I can do this!* when preachers expound on the necessity to read our Bibles and give to the poor. But therein lies the problem. As soon as we discover we can't "do it," those feelings of guilt so burden us that we can no longer experience the benefits of relationship with God. Legalism can seem pretty, and with it being so subtly and often taught from the pulpit, most of us don't even recognize it. We don't see its ugly end-result until we begin experiencing the emotions of guilt and condemnation that follow it (Rom. 7:10).

The law speaks. It acts like an alarm system to our conscience. If you have an alarm system in your home, it alerts you if an intruder tries to break in to your house. That's its job. But the alarm won't go off if an intruder tries to break in to your neighbor's house—that's not where it is installed. The alarm system is like the law. It only triggers your conscience (and produces the guilt that says, "You've messed up again") if it is installed in your belief system. The law speaks, but only to the person committed to and living under its rule-keeping system.

Paul says that any person who tries to earn the love, acceptance, forgiveness, or favor of a perfect, righteous, and holy God is going to experience guilt and condemnation. In our own strength, we simply are not capable of living up to God's standard. And our consciences have no trouble pointing that out! As a matter of fact, that was the law's purpose.

> *Now we know that whatsoever things the law says, it says to them who are under the law: that every mouth may be stopped, and all the world may become guilty before God.*
>
> *Romans 3:19 (KJV 2000)*

> *But before faith came, we were kept in custody under the law, being shut up to the faith which was later to be revealed. ²⁴Therefore the Law has become our tutor to lead us to Christ, so that we may be justified by faith. ²⁵But now that faith has come, we are no*

longer under a tutor. ²⁶For you are all sons of God through faith in Christ Jesus.

Galatians 3:23-26 (NASB)

As I said earlier, the law was a contract between God and man. It said, "If you do this, then God will do that." And like any contract, if someone broke it, there were consequences to pay. Now if you and I made a business arrangement and signed a contract, that contract would stipulate the terms and conditions of our agreement. It would tell us what we had to do to fulfill the contract to get our agreed upon reward. It would also tell us what consequences or penalties would be incurred if we didn't fulfill our part of the deal. The thing with contracts, though, is that unless we spell out an expiration date or include a "nullification clause" as part of

When Christ came, He fulfilled our contract with God.

the penalties, our contract would keep going (reiterating the requirements and accruing the consequences) even if one of us broke it. The only way to remove that contract from between us is to fulfill it. What we forget is that Christ came to fulfill the law.

Think not that I am come to destroy the law, or the prophets: I am not come to destroy, but to fulfil. ¹⁸For verily I say unto you, Till heaven and earth pass, one jot or one tittle shall in no wise pass from the law, till all be fulfilled.

Matthew 5:17-18 (KJV)

When Christ came, He fulfilled our contract with God. It is no longer a factor in our relationship (Col.

2:14). Jesus met all the law's requirements and, according to Hebrews, enacted a new covenant with God—a better one!

> *But as it now is, He [Christ] has acquired a [priestly] ministry which is as much superior and more excellent [than the old] as the covenant (the agreement) of which He is the Mediator (the Arbiter, Agent) is superior and more excellent, [because] it is enacted and rests upon more important (sublimer, higher, and nobler) promises.*
>
> *Hebrews 8:6*

There is nothing you or I can do to affect this covenant. Even though we are listed as beneficiaries, this covenant has nothing to do with us. That is why it's superior—it is between Jesus and God. For when *"He saw that there was no one to intervene; His own arm achieved salvation for Him, and His own righteousness sustained Him."* (Is. 59:16)

> **We must not lose focus on the finished work of the cross and attempt to please God with our own efforts.**

We must not lose focus on the finished work of the cross and attempt to please God with our own efforts. Doing this, Paul said, invalidates Christ's work in our lives. It rejects what He died to accomplish and plunges us back into the defectiveness of the old covenant.

> *Stand fast therefore in the liberty wherewith Christ hath made us free, and be not entangled again with*

the yoke of bondage. ²Behold, I Paul say unto you, that if ye be circumcised, Christ shall profit you nothing. ³For I testify again to every man that is circumcised, that he is a debtor to do the whole law. ⁴Christ is become of no effect unto you, whosoever of you are justified by the law; ye are fallen from grace.

Galatians 5:1-4 (KJV)

Paul must have been serious about this concept to repeat himself in this way. He even says, "When you attempt to live by your own religious plans, you are cut off from Christ and fallen from grace." Do we realize how serious that is? (Now I know some of you are feeling guilty for feeling guilty, so let me stop for a moment and say this: Grace is God's undeserved goodness towards us. But it is also His ability in our lives. So the phrase "fallen from grace" literally means we've fallen from God's ability back to our own. Can we return to His grace? Absolutely—that is what grace is all about.) But the moment we think there's something we have to do (or abstain from) in order to keep God happy, we put ourselves back under the law.

It doesn't have to be circumcision like Paul noted. (That's just the issue the Galatians were dealing with in his day.) It could be fasting or Bible reading or prayer. It might be keeping the Ten Commandments or witnessing. Or it could be something that doesn't even come from the Bible. It might be something you came up with (like voting Republican)—or something your church or society-at-large came up with (like drinking or speeding). Anything that says "in order to be a good Christian, I must…" is a rule-keeping system. And Paul says the idea of serving God by upholding the law or any rule-keeping system is ridiculous. Besides the fact that no man can live "good enough" to earn the attention of God. The attitude that says, "I have to at least try to live up to God's standard," actually squanders the free gift of Christ. Let's look at Galatians again, this time in the Message Bible.

> *Christ has set us free to live a free life. So take your stand! Never again let anyone put a harness of slavery on you. I am emphatic about this. The moment any one of you submits to circumcision or any other rule-keeping system, at that same moment Christ's hard-won gift of freedom is squandered. I repeat my warning: The person who accepts the ways of circumcision trades all the advantages of the free life in Christ for the obligations of the slave life of the law. I suspect you would never intend this, but this is what happens. When you attempt to live by your own religious plans and projects, you are cut off from Christ, you fall out of grace.*
>
> *Galatians 5:1-4 (MSG)*

Walking in Grace

There is no more rule-keeping system between us and God. In fact, just before Jesus died, He cried out, "It is finished." (John 19:30) In that moment, not only was the old covenant of works fulfilled and annulled, but a new one that is by faith was signed in blood. The new covenant that we are beneficiaries of does not resemble the old one. Hebrews 8:9 says this new covenant is "Not like the covenant that I made with their fathers on the day when I took them by the hand to lead them out of the land of Egypt." It isn't founded upon our performance of the Ten Commandments. It is founded upon the law of Christ. That law is a law of life (Rom. 8:2), a law of liberty (James 1:25), and a law of faith (Rom. 3:27-28). It is the law that God writes on our own hearts so we can live from the heart—as His people.

> *This is the covenant I will make with the people of Israel after that time," declares the LORD. "I will put my law in their minds and write it on their hearts. I will be their God, and they will be my people.*
> *Jeremiah 31:33 (NIV)*

How is that different than mere performance? Now the things we do, we do with a clear conscience, knowing that our actions do not change God's opinion of us. Now we live life in the middle of His grace, allowing our lives to become a reflection of His. Are there still rules and laws that we obey? In regard to our relationship with other people or society in general, yes. We still need to respect the speed limit and follow the rules at our workplaces; otherwise, we can't function within society. But our obedience or disobedience of those rules does not affect our relationship with God—it may affect our relationship with people, but not with God. Is there still need for discipline? Again, the disciplines we erect in our lives aren't evil; they can serve a good purpose. (For example, the discipline of not overeating serves the purpose of keeping our bodies healthy so they can be the blessing to us that God intended them to be.) But those disciplines, and our successes or failures in them, do not change our relationship with God.

Understanding how God sees us produces confidence before Him. First John says, "Beloved, if our heart does not convict us [of guilt], we have confidence [complete assurance and boldness] before God." (I John 3:21) We know that regardless of whether or not we feel we deserve it, He is faithful to His Word.

> *Therefore, believers, since we have confidence and full freedom to enter the Holy Place [the place where God dwells] by [means of] the blood of Jesus, ²⁰by this new and living way which He initiated and opened for us through the veil [as in the Holy of Holies], that is, through His flesh, ²¹and since we have a great and wonderful Priest [Who rules] over the house of God, ²²let us approach [God] with a true and sincere heart in unqualified assurance of faith, having had our hearts sprinkled clean from an evil conscience and our bodies washed with pure water. ²³Let us seize and hold tightly the confession of our hope without wavering, for He who promised is reliable and trustworthy and faithful [to His word].*

> *Hebrews 10:19-23*

Did you know that the Greek word translated as holy in our Bibles is actually the word *hagios*, which literally means *"set apart"*? In early Christian writings, it referred to "being different" from the world and meant we "exclusively belonged to God." And the word translated as perfect *(teleios)* isn't talking about being blameless in our moral behavior. It actually means *"having reached its end-goal; complete."* It is talking about having peace, being made whole, and becoming perfectly innocent (Archer and Hill, 1987). Unfortunately, over the years, the meaning of those words has morphed into something very different. But what Jesus accomplished for us has not. Christ set us apart to belong exclusively to God. He completed God's plan of relationship and brought us to His end-goal! From God's perspective, we are as holy as we are ever going to be.

So, in light of all that God has done for us, what do we do? Do we have a responsibility toward Him? Shouldn't we feel obligated to serve Him or "repay" Him for what He has done? I'll discuss this more in-depth later, but New Testament responsibility is simply this: "a decision to respond to His ability." Responding to God's ability—to Grace—looks like this: Suppose someone wrote out a million dollar check with your name on it. They told you about it and left it sitting on their desk for you to pick up at your earliest convenience. It would be exciting to get that kind of news, but that check would do you no good just sitting on their desk. You would have to believe what they said was true and put forth the effort to get in your car and go pick it up. What happens once you've got that million-dollar-check in your hands? Nothing—until you deposit it in the bank. Again, you have to believe that the person who gave you the check has the means to back it up, and you must put forth the effort to get yourself to the bank, lay that check in front of the teller, give them your ID, and deposit it. Now you've got a million dollars sitting in your account! But again, that money isn't going to do you any good until you go to the ATM and draw some money out of your account.

Let us never stray from that revelation and fall from God's ability back onto our own.

But even after all that "work" would you tell someone, "I just earned a million dollars today!"? Of course not! You didn't earn that money. You didn't work for it. You just responded to it!

As we learn to rest in God's grace and establish within

ourselves the finished work of Christ, we will respond as did Paul, "There is only one thing I want to know for the rest of my life, Jesus Christ and God's demonstration of love toward me by His cross!" (1 Cor. 2:2) Let us never stray from that revelation and fall from God's ability back onto our own. Let us remember, "**It is finished!**"

Chapter Five

FULLY PERSUADED

All of us are in different stages of our journey and growth in the revelation of righteousness. While we may mentally assent to the fact that Jesus' death and resurrection put us in right standing with God, we must all learn to continually walk out that reality in our day-to-day lives. In some areas, we may find ourselves fully persuaded of this truth. In others, we may need to consciously work on establishing this truth in our hearts. Because the only way we can completely rid ourselves of the feelings of guilt and condemnation that accompany our relationship with God is to become fully persuaded of what Christ accomplished for us on the cross.

Look at the fruit of your life. If you are struggling with guilt or addiction, if you have a financial or relationship problem, those may be clues that you do not really understand this foundational truth. You may not be fully convinced that God loves and accepts you, that He is pleased with you, and that He desires good for your life—including intimate relationship with Him. You may not yet truly believe that you have been made right before God (Rom. 2:13). You may not consider yourself holy even though Hebrews 10:10 declares, "And in accordance with this will [of God] we [who believe in the message of salvation] have been sanctified [that is, set apart as holy for God and His purposes] through the offering of the body of Jesus Christ (the Messiah, the Anointed) once for all." You see the person who does not know they've been made holy will continue to act as if they are unholy. But when you become established in the fact that you **are** holy, you **are** right with God, you will start acting like it, and the fruit of that understanding will begin to spill out and show itself in every area of your life.

Does that mean you will never make another mistake or that you will never miss the mark or sin again? No. At some point or another, you will violate your conscience; you will hurt someone with your words or disappoint them with your actions. When that happens, seek forgiveness from the person you wronged, and try to make it right so you can live at peace and keep your mistakes from becoming an issue in your relationship with them (Rom. 12:17-21). But know that your mistake, your sin, will **never** become an issue between you and God. Jesus has taken care of that issue permanently! (Heb. 10:14) He has completely removed your sin and signed a covenant of peace between you and God!

For a brief moment I forsook you, but with great compassion and mercy I will gather you [to Me] again. ⁸In a little burst of wrath I hid My face from you for a moment, but with age-enduring love and kindness I will have compassion and mercy on you, says the Lord, your Redeemer. [9] For this is like the days of Noah to Me; as I swore that the waters of Noah should no more go over the earth, so have I sworn that I will not be angry with you or rebuke you. [10] For though the mountains should depart and the hills be shaken or removed, yet My love and kindness shall not depart from you, nor shall My covenant of peace and completeness be removed, says the Lord, Who has compassion on you.

Isaiah 54:7-10

Recognize Your Sinlessness

Your sin is not hiding under the desk waiting for an opportune moment to revisit you and shout to God that you are "unclean." It isn't attached to your hip hoping to trip you up when you aren't looking so you can't enter God's presence. It's not even buried in your heart trying to dig its way out. Your sin has been removed.

For as the heaven is high above the earth, so great is his mercy toward them that fear him. [12] As far as the east is from the west, so far hath he removed our transgressions from us.

Psalm 103:11-12 (KJV)

Then why do I feel as if sin is plaguing my life and relationship with God, Arthur? Because you've convinced yourself that it is. Every week you go to church and listen to a preacher expound on the horrors of sin. You go to Bible study and read about ferreting sin out of your life. You talk to your Christian friends and tell them to pray for

Sister So-and-so who's really struggling with such-and-such sin. Then you go to prayer meetings and pray, "God, our nation has sinned. Forgive us and have mercy on us even though we don't deserve it. Save us for the sake of the righteous just like you told Abraham you would save Sodom. Forgive my city for straying so far from You. Expose evil and shine the light of your salvation on us. Forgive my family, Lord. Forgive me God. Without You, I'm hopeless. Every day I fail You. Forgive me God. Deliver me from my sin!" Do you not realize you have filled every part of your Christian life with consciousness of sin? You have elevated God's standard of perfection, but forgotten that Jesus reached that standard and gave you the credit!

> *The penalty you deserved has been cancelled, and God has not heard an accusation against you for 2000 years!*

But [the words], It was credited to him, were written not for his sake alone, ²⁴But [they were written] for our sakes too. [Righteousness, standing acceptable to God] will be granted and credited to us also who believe in (trust in, adhere to, and rely on) God, Who raised Jesus our Lord from the dead, ²⁵Who was betrayed and put to death because of our misdeeds and was raised to secure our justification (our acquittal), [making our account balance and absolving us from all guilt before God].

Romans 4:23-25

For by one offering he hath perfected for ever them that are sanctified...¹⁹Having therefore, brethren, boldness to enter into the holiest by the blood of Jesus...²²Let us draw near with a true heart in full assurance of faith, having our hearts sprinkled from an evil conscience, and our bodies washed with pure water.

Hebrews 10:14, 19, 22 (KJV)

Because of Jesus' sacrifice, you have received absolute and eternal forgiveness of your sin. The penalty you deserved has been cancelled, and God has not heard an accusation against you for 2000 years! (Rom. 8:33) That means, if you're reading this book (I'm assuming you're less than 2000 years old), none of your failings—not a single one—has *ever* been brought before God for condemnation and judgment!

But aren't we all going to face God's judgment, Arthur? Scripture says, *"It is appointed for all men once to die, and after that, the judgment."* (Heb. 9:27) Yes, but it goes on to say:

Even so it is that Christ, having been offered to take upon Himself and bear as a burden the sins of many once and once for all, will appear a second time, not to carry any burden of sin nor to deal with sin, but to bring to full salvation those who are [eagerly, constantly, and patiently] waiting for and expecting Him.

Hebrews 9:28

That's the judgment of God. Jesus is going to come back, but He will never have to deal with sin again. He is coming to bring about full salvation for everyone that believes. On that day, God will judge all believers innocent in Christ—forgiven (Col. 1:13-14). Without Jesus, we would be condemned, but praise God, we are not without Jesus! If you feel disconnected to God or unworthy to receive from Him, I assure you the problem is only in your own mind. Colossians chapter one tells us:

> *For it pleased the Father that in him should all fulness dwell; ²⁰And, having made peace through the blood of his cross, by him to reconcile all things unto himself; by him, I say, whether they be things in earth, or things in heaven. ²¹And you, that were sometime alienated and enemies in your mind by wicked works, yet now hath he reconciled ²²In the body of his flesh through death, to present you holy and unblameable and unreproveable in his sight: ²³If ye continue in the faith grounded and settled, and be not moved away from the hope of the gospel, which ye have heard, and which was preached to every creature which is under heaven.*
>
> *Colossians 1:19-23 (KJV)*

Notice Paul says, "it pleased God" that Christ would die on the cross so that you and I "who were enemies of God and alienated from Him **in our minds**" might be reconciled. Alienated means to *"feel you no longer belong."* (Merriam Webster, 2015) It would include situations like divorce and self-banishment. Before Christ, we were separated from God—not because He was so mean or demanding—but because we felt guilty, and our guilt drove us from Him. We divorced (completely separated) ourselves from God's life, God's blessings, God's presence, and became an enemy of His in our own minds and thinking. Sin changed the things we thought and believed about God.

When we looked at Jesus' suffering, we saw Him "smitten and stricken of God" like Isaiah said in Isaiah 53:4. We thought God was mad, but in reality, He was dealing with sin like a skillful surgeon. If a surgeon needed to remove a cancer from the body, he would carefully and precisely cut it out. He wouldn't go hacking around the body out of anger or disgust against the cancer. Every move he made would be predetermined and ordered to give life back to that body. God dealt with sin in Christ's body the same way. His intent was to not only cleanse us of sin, but also of

Jesus came to save us from ourselves, not from God!

a guilty conscience. He wanted to open up the way for real relationship with us again.

Change Your Picture of God

Jesus came to save us from ourselves, not from God! John 3:16 says, "For God so **loved** the world…" It doesn't say, "For God was so angry with the world…" I know people don't often preach it, but God has never moved from His position of love and relationship. Hebrews tells us that He is the "same yesterday, today, and forever." (vs. 13:8) Jesus didn't come so God wouldn't have to be ticked off at us anymore. He came to change our minds about who God is.

No man has ever seen God at any time; the only unique Son, or the only begotten God, Who is in the bosom [in the intimate presence] of the Father, He has declared Him [He has revealed Him and brought Him out where He can be seen; He has interpreted Him and He has made Him known].

John 1:18

Before Jesus came, we didn't have a true picture of who God is. People saw Him as God Almighty, others, the God-Who-Knows-Everything. Some saw Him only as a God of Justice. Still others as a God of Mercy. The Old Testament writers themselves didn't accurately know God. They never fully comprehended God or saw Him for Who He really is, and thus struggled to portray Him clearly. *What about Abraham and Moses?* You say. *They saw God.* They may have had encounters or interactions with God, but they never really knew Him. They only saw Him for who they believed Him to be. That's why John said, "Only Jesus—who has been intimately involved with the Father—has seen Him. Only He can reveal or interpret His character."

Hebrews also says:

In many separate revelations [each of which set forth a portion of the Truth] and in different ways God spoke of old to [our] forefathers in and by the prophets, [2][But] in the last of these days He has spoken to us in [the person of a] Son, Whom He appointed Heir and lawful Owner of all things, also by and through Whom He created the worlds and the reaches of space and the ages of time [He made, produced, built, operated, and arranged them in order]. [3]He is the sole expression of the glory of God [the Light-being, the [out-raying or radiance of the divine], and He is the perfect imprint and very image of [God's] nature, upholding and maintaining and guiding and propelling the universe by His mighty word of power. When He had by offering Himself accomplished our cleansing of sins and riddance of guilt, He sat down at the right hand of the divine Majesty on high.
Hebrews 1:1-3

The author of Hebrews is saying that there were many separate revelations of God in the Old Testament, but each was only a portion of the truth. Trying to see God in the Old Testament was like trying to see an entire picture with only one or two pieces of a puzzle. The true picture of God is only found in the father-son relationship between Him and Christ. God is a Father. For all eternity, God is Father, Son, and Holy Spirit. He has always lived in the context of relationship, and He will not deviate from that.

So I charge you, don't make opinions or assumptions about God and His attitude towards you without first looking

Don't continue to live "alienated in your own mind."

at Jesus. Don't continue to live "alienated in your own mind." I know it takes effort, but change your thinking, and become fully persuaded of and established in His love for you. Just remember the effort you dispense isn't spent on doing what's right, it's consumed on believing what's right.

Take scripture and the revelations you get from this book of all that Christ accomplished for you, and meditate on them. Speak them over your life, and persuade your heart of their truth. Become like Paul, "fully persuaded" of God's love (Rom. 8:38-39). Understand that the blood of Jesus offers assurance that there is no other sacrifice necessary to atone for sin. There is no more penance, no more offering, no more vows or consecrations necessary for you to become right with God.

Yet we know that a man is not justified [and placed in right standing with God] by works of the Law, but [only] through faith in [God's beloved Son,] Christ Jesus. And even we [as Jews] have believed in Christ Jesus, so that we may be justified by faith in Christ and not by works of the Law. By observing the Law no one will ever be justified [declared free of the guilt of sin and its penalty].

Galatians 2:16

Surrender to Grace

Persuasion is a process in surrender. When Paul first met Christ on that road to Damascus, he described himself as "head and shoulders above his peers" in regard to the law (Gal. 1:13-16 MSG). But Paul still had something to learn about Grace—the message God called him to preach. He actually disappeared from church history for about ten to fourteen years, and when he resurfaced in Antioch, Paul began preaching a message that nobody had ever heard. Paul had to surrender all his past achievements (and failures) to the cause of Christ and allow the truth of God's grace to reestablish his belief system (Phil. 3:13). Only then did he begin making an eternal difference and living the type of life God created him for.

But I'm not qualified like Paul. I'm still struggling to believe! The good news is we aren't qualified based on our own performance; we are qualified based upon Christ's work.

Then said Jesus unto his disciples, If any man will come after me, let him deny himself, and take up his cross, and follow me. ²⁵For whosoever will save his life shall lose it: and whosoever will lose his life for my sake shall find it. ²⁶For what is a man profited, if he shall gain the whole world, and lose his own soul? or what shall a man give in exchange for his soul? ²⁷For the Son of man shall come in the glory of his Father with his angels; and then he shall reward every man according to his works.

Matthew 16:24-27 (KJV)

I looked up that word "works" and discovered it's not plural! According to the Greek Lexicon, the original Greek word *praxis,* used in verse 27, is a singular noun (Thayer, 2002). This verse isn't saying that God will reward every man according to that man's works (plural verb). It says every man will be rewarded according to His work (singular noun)—meaning Jesus' accomplishment! Jesus' work became our reward!

Does that mean we can throw God's standard of living out the window? No. Peter said, "Think clearly and exercise self-control...live as God's obedient children, and don't return to the old ways" of living or thinking (1 Pet. 1:13-14 NLT). Why not? Is God going to get angry? Will He give up on us? No. Peter is saying that kind of living is stupid. Do you have children? When you give your children rules or want them to live to a certain standard, is it to make you look good? Is it to keep you happy? No. You give them rules to protect them. Really, that's what Peter is saying. If we fail to live righteously, our misdeeds don't contaminate God, but they do cause us pain, guilt, and sorrow. When we choose to follow God's standard and live righteously (applying the Ten Commandments to our earthly relationships), we aren't doing it to make God look good or to keep Him happy.

We live righteously to keep ourselves from the pain and sorrow sin causes.

> *...Christ brought you over to God's side and put your lives together, whole and holy in his presence. You don't walk away from a gift like that! You stay grounded and steady in that bond of trust, constantly tuned in to the Message, careful not to be distracted or diverted. There is no other Message—just this one.*
> *Colossians 1:22-23 (MSG)*

> *So roll up your sleeves, put your mind in gear, be totally ready to receive the gift that's coming when Jesus arrives. Don't lazily slip back into those old grooves of evil, doing just what you feel like doing. You didn't know any better then; you do now. As obedient children, let yourselves be pulled into a way of life shaped by God's life, a life energetic and blazing with holiness. God said, "I am holy; you be holy." 1*
> *Peter 1:13-16 (MSG)*

We should never want to return to our old way of living. Sin only produces fear, shame, guilt, and death. God's way—the way of obedience—is much better! His way produces life and peace (Rom. 8:6). But what exactly does obedience entail? Someone asked Jesus that question in John chapter six. He answered, "This is the work of God, that you believe in the One he has sent." (John 6:29) We must become fully persuaded that all we need to do to please God is to believe in His Son, Jesus the Christ, and surrender to the work He came to perform.

Part Three

UNDER NO OBLIGATION

*Any person you feel obligated to,
you will learn to hate.*

Chapter Six

HIS WORK, OUR REWARD

Jesus Christ is the only way to relationship with God. There is no other name, no other offering, no other way to cleanse sin or remove guilt (Acts 4:12, Heb. 1:3). Without Jesus, we all stand before God condemned and awaiting death. In our sinful state, without Jesus, our minds tell us we can't approach God; we are His enemies and deserving of condemnation. But brothers and sisters, I have good news—**we are not without Jesus!** The apostle Paul said, "And you, that were sometime alienated and enemies in your mind by wicked works, yet now hath he reconciled." (Col. 1:21 KJV)

One of the most awesome powers of the finished work of Christ is that we were not only declared forgiven, but were made perfectly innocent before God in and through the death, burial, and resurrection of Jesus Christ! Jesus died to cleanse us and clear our record of all sin. He was raised for our justification and is now seated at the right hand of God, eternally sealing our acceptance into His family (Heb. 2:11).

Let's not cheapen what Christ accomplished.

But many people feel what He accomplished only balanced the scales of justice. Many liken Jesus' work to Adam's failings—only in the positive—and say that what Adam lost, Jesus regained and returned to us as God's children. But Romans says:

> God's free gift is not at all to be compared to the trespass **[His grace is out of all proportion to the fall of man]**. For if many died through one man's falling away (his lapse, his offense), much more profusely did God's grace and the free gift [that comes] through the undeserved favor of the one Man Jesus Christ abound and overflow to and for [the benefit of] many. ¹⁶Nor is the free gift at all to be compared to the effect of that one [man's] sin. For the sentence [following the trespass] of one [man] brought condemnation, whereas the free gift [following] many transgressions brings justification (an act of righteousness).
>
> *Romans 5:15-16*

Let's not cheapen what Christ accomplished. Jesus didn't just balance the scales of God's justice; He completely tipped them in our favor! Remember, the Old Covenant required a blood sacrifice to cover sin, but that sacrifice couldn't remove sin or its consequence of guilt and shame. In order for the New Covenant to accomplish more, there had to be a far better or greater sacrifice.

> [In fact] under the Law almost everything is purified

by means of blood, and without the shedding of blood there is neither release from sin and its guilt nor the remission of the due and merited punishment for sins. [23]By such means, therefore, it was necessary for the [earthly] copies of the heavenly things to be purified, but the actual heavenly things themselves [required far] better and nobler sacrifices than these. [24]For Christ (the Messiah) has not entered into a sanctuary made with [human] hands, only a copy and pattern and type of the true one, but [He has entered] into heaven itself, now to appear in the [very] presence of God on our behalf.

Hebrews 9:22-24

Notice what verse 24 of Hebrews nine says. "For Christ (the Messiah) has not entered into a sanctuary made with [human] hands, only a copy and pattern and type of the true one, but [He has entered] into heaven itself, now to appear in the [very] presence of God on our behalf." Jesus stood before God on our behalf. That literally means, *"as us."* He didn't just come to earth and appear before God as our advocate. He didn't just come to God with a list of our names like an attorney representing his clients. Jesus entered heaven, appearing in the very presence of God, **as us** (as if it were you and I standing before God), and there He restored our ability to have relationship with God. Jesus was not detached from us during His work. He became a human being so that He could be the substitute for every man, woman, and child who ever lived or ever will live on this planet. Jesus substituted His life, His righteousness, for ours.

Therefore, it was necessary for him to be made in every respect like us, his brothers and sisters, so that he could be our merciful and faithful High Priest before God. Then he could offer a sacrifice that would take away the sins of the people.

Hebrews 2:17 (NLT)

This High Priest of ours understands our weaknesses, for he faced all of the same testings we do, yet he did not sin.

Hebrews 4:15 (NLT)

I'm not downplaying Adam's fall. Sin was a big, big deal. Adam's sin was like someone driving over a fire hydrant with water gushing out all over the place. That's not something you can drive away from or cover up and hope no one notices. Sin affected all of us in a big way; it tipped the scales of God's justice in a way that no one could rebalance. But by comparison, God's grace, demonstrated towards us in Christ's finished work on the cross, was like Niagara Falls (from which 750,000 gallons of water flows every second). It's incomparable to that little fire hydrant! Jesus' work didn't just tip the scales back and give us a clean slate to start over with; it completely obliterated them!

The Unfairness of the Gospel

Christianity (relationship with God through Christ) has never been about what is fair. It's always been about a Father's love for His children. Jesus' life and death exchanged what the law instituted (relationship based on performance) with a new covenant of Grace (relationship based on Him). Now we have access to God and receive all the benefits of an intimate relationship with Him through Jesus' blood. Jesus did the work; we got the reward!

*For if because of one man's trespass (lapse, offense)
death reigned through that one, much more surely
will those who receive [God's] overflowing grace
(unmerited favor) and the free gift of righteousness
[putting them into right standing with Himself]
reign as kings in life through the one Man Jesus
Christ (the Messiah, the Anointed One).*

Romans 5:17

The problem many of us have is that we have been
lead to believe that we should still feel guilty even after
trusting that Jesus, once for all, fully paid for and dealt
with our sin. The truth is that Jesus' finished work not
only dealt with our sin, but it also cleansed us from an
evil guilty conscience! The writer of Hebrews says it this
way:

*The Son is the radiance and only expression of
the glory of [our awesome] God [reflecting God's
Shekinah glory, the Light-being, the brilliant
light of the divine], and the exact representation
and perfect imprint of His [Father's] essence, and
upholding and maintaining and propelling all
things [the entire physical and spiritual universe]
by His powerful word [carrying the universe along
to its predetermined goal]. When He [Himself and
no other] had [by offering Himself on the cross as
a sacrifice for sin] accomplished purification from
sins and established our freedom from guilt, He sat
down [revealing His completed work] at the right
hand of the Majesty on high [revealing His Divine
authority].*

Hebrews 1:3

Many believers are still struggling to come to grips
with this truth. Jesus' sacrifice not only dealt with our sin,

but (once accepted and fully believed in our hearts) His work on the cross also possesses the power to rid us of all guilt! Declaring us not only *forgiven* before God, but also *perfectly innocent* in our own hearts and minds. The Living Bible says it this way, *"...He is the one who died to cleanse us and clear our record of all sin."*

I've found that many Christians readily assent to the fact that Jesus' sacrifice dealt with the sin issue between God and man. But most do not hold the ultimate resolve that not only is sin no longer an issue between God and man, but it is no longer an issue between man and God. You see, Christ's death and resurrection was not just an appeasement of the hostility toward man in the mind and heart of God, but it was also an appeasement of the guilt and hostility toward God in the hearts and minds of men. This is beautifully illustrated in Hebrews:

> *For since the Law has only a shadow [just a pale representation] of the good things to come—not the very image of those things—it can never, by offering the same sacrifices continually year after year, make perfect those who approach [its altars]. ²For if it were otherwise, would not these sacrifices have stopped being offered? For the worshipers, having once [for all time] been cleansed, would no longer have a consciousness of sin.*
>
> *³But [as it is] these [continual] sacrifices bring a fresh reminder of sins [to be atoned for] year after year, ⁴for it is impossible for the blood of bulls and goats to take away sins. ⁵Therefore, when Christ enters into the world, He says, "Sacrifice and offering You have not desired, but [instead] You have prepared a body for Me [to offer]; ⁶In burnt offerings and sacrifices for sin You have taken no delight. ⁷"Then I said, 'Behold, I*

have come to do Your will, O God—[To fulfill] what is written of Me in the scroll of the book.'" ⁸After saying [in the citation] above, "You have neither desired, nor have You taken delight in sacrifices and offerings and whole burnt offerings and sacrifices for sin" (which are offered according to the Law) ⁹then He said, "Behold, I have come to do Your will." [And so] He does away with the first [covenant as a means of atoning for sin based on animal sacrifices] so that He may inaugurate and establish the second [covenant by means of obedience].

¹⁰And in accordance with this will [of God] we [who believe in the message of salvation] have been sanctified [that is, set apart as holy for God and His purposes] through the offering of the body of Jesus Christ (the Messiah, the Anointed) once for all. ¹¹Every priest stands [at his altar of service] ministering daily, offering the same sacrifices over and over, which are never able to strip away sins [that envelop and cover us]; ¹²whereas Christ, having offered the one sacrifice [the all-sufficient sacrifice of Himself] for sins for all time, sat down [signifying the completion of atonement for sin] at the right hand of God [the position of honor], ¹³waiting from that time onward until his enemies are made a footstool for His feet.

¹⁴For by the one offering He has perfected forever and completely cleansed those who are being sanctified [bringing each believer to spiritual completion and maturity]. ¹⁵And the Holy Spirit also adds His testimony to us [in confirmation of this]; for after having said, ¹⁶"This is the covenant that I will make with them after those days, says the Lord: I will imprint My laws upon their heart, and on their mind I will inscribe them [producing an inward change],"

He then says, ¹⁷"And their sins and their lawless acts I will remember no more [no longer holding their sins against them]." ¹⁸Now where there is [absolute] forgiveness and complete cancellation of the penalty of these things, there is no longer any offering [to be made to atone] for sin.

¹⁹Therefore, believers, since we have confidence and full freedom to enter the Holy Place [the place where God dwells] by [means of] the blood of Jesus, ²⁰by this new and living way which He initiated and opened for us through the veil [as in the Holy of Holies], that is, through His flesh, ²¹and since we have a great and wonderful Priest [Who rules] over the house of God, ²²let us approach [God] with a true and sincere heart in unqualified assurance of faith, having had our hearts sprinkled clean from an evil conscience and our bodies washed with pure water. ²³Let us seize and hold tightly the confession of our hope without wavering, for He who promised is reliable and trustworthy and faithful [to His word].

Hebrews 10:1-23

Remember what I said about the word "perfect" in your Bible? It's not talking about being morally perfect or sinless, but about wholeness and completeness. In other words, we have been made completely and perfectly innocent by the blood of Christ. And notice how the writer continues by stating that if a sacrifice existed that had the ability to take away sin, there would no longer be any consciousness or

> **...we have been made completely and perfectly innocent by the blood of Christ.**

perception of sin and the guilt it causes. Remember again, the word "consciousness" is talking about a knowing or awareness of something. You see, the writer of Hebrews starts out these verses by creating a premise for something he is going to later reveal. He is making a case for the sacrificial work of Christ that cleansed and perfected every believer once and for all eternity.

This truth means that every believer today should no longer live in the realm of debilitating guilt and consciousness of sin. Just like God has no remembrance of our sin (as we discussed in Chapter Three), we should no longer allow our sins, failings, and guilt to rob us of the benefits of our relationship with Him. Because of the sacrifice of Jesus, we have absolute and eternal forgiveness of sin. The blood of Christ assures us that there is no need to make any other sacrifice to atone for our sin or remove the penalty of our lawbreaking.

Forgiveness—Guaranteed!

You see, the blood of Jesus not only cleansed us of all sin, but if we fully believe, trust in, and rely on the power and virtue of that blood, it will rid us of a guilty conscience and allow us to live life as kings (victorious, wise, prosperous, and strong). The writer of Hebrews calls a guilty conscience an "evil conscience." (There is nothing holy, spiritual, or godly about guilt! It is plain and simply **evil**.) First Corinthians tells us that Jesus has established us and ensures our strength and vindication to the end of time.

That you are not [consciously] falling behind or lacking

in any special spiritual endowment or Christian grace [[a]the reception of which is due to the power of divine grace operating in your souls by the Holy Spirit], while you wait and watch [constantly living in hope] for the coming of our Lord Jesus Christ and [His] being made visible to all. ⁸And He will establish you to the end [keep you steadfast, give you strength, and guarantee your vindication; He will be your warrant against all accusation or indictment so that you will be] guiltless and irreproachable in the day of our Lord Jesus Christ (the Messiah).
1 Corinthians 1:7-8

Jesus is our guarantee! I remember when Cathy and I first immigrated to America. It was fun setting up house again and discovering how our tastes had changed since we were first married. But my favorite part was buying new appliances. We would go into a big-box retailer, decide on a brand and color, and be informed that the particular appliance we were considering came with a manufacturer's one-year limited warranty. Then at checkout we learned we could extend our warranty for up to nine months. "And as always, you have our 90-day, no-questions-asked return policy."

"What?! Are you serious?" I asked. That was the greatest thing I'd ever heard! In South Africa, warranties were unheard of. If you're lucky, you might get ninety minutes to change your mind about a purchase and bring it back. But everything in America comes with warranties—new cars, appliances, TVs, construction services, even garden plants—it's great.

A warranty guarantees that what I'm purchasing will be defect-free for a specified length of time. (Having lived without warranties for most of my life, I don't take them for granted. Every time I'm offered a warranty, I take it. I read it. And when necessary, I stand on it until I get my new product.) But nearly all the warranties I've seen are limited. Have you noticed that? The manufacturer only promises to fix or replace their product for a specified length of time, they only work with the original purchaser, and they won't fix something that can't be proven as "their fault." But according to First Corinthians, Jesus is our guarantee, and His warranty is limitless! He "will establish you to the end [keep you steadfast, give you strength, and guarantee your vindication; He will be your warrant against all accusation or indictment so that you will be] guiltless and irreproachable" to the end (vs. 7). We will go through life, we will make mistakes, people may point fingers at us, we may feel guilty, but Jesus is our warrant against every accusation! His blood guarantees our vindication before God for all time!

> *Now it is God who makes both us and you stand firm in Christ. He anointed us,[22] set his seal of ownership on us, and put his Spirit in our hearts as a deposit, guaranteeing what is to come.*
> *2 Corinthians 1:21-22 (NIV)*

Even if we experience negative circumstances, nothing that happens in our lives is an indication that God has accepted an accusation against us or has distanced Himself from us. I like what Paul said in the book of Romans:

> *What then shall we say to all these things? If God is for us, who can be [successful] against us? [32]He who did not spare [even] His own Son, but gave Him up for us all, how will He not also, along with*

Him, graciously give us all things? ³³Who will bring any charge against God's elect (His chosen ones)? It is God who justifies us [declaring us blameless and putting us in a right relationship with Himself]. ³⁴Who is the one who condemns us? Christ Jesus is the One who died [to pay our penalty], and more than that, who was raised [from the dead], and who is at the right hand of God interceding [with the Father] for us. ³⁵Who shall ever separate us from the love of Christ? Will tribulation, or distress, or persecution, or famine, or nakedness, or danger, or sword? ³⁶Just as it is written and forever remains written, "For Your sake we are put to death all day long; we are regarded as sheep for the slaughter."³⁷Yet in all these things we are more than conquerors and gain an overwhelming victory through Him who loved us [so much that He died for us]. ³⁸For I am convinced [and continue to be convinced—beyond any doubt] that neither death, nor life, nor angels, nor principalities, nor things present and threatening, nor things to come, nor powers, ³⁹nor height, nor depth, nor any other created thing, will be able to separate us from the [unlimited] love of God, which is in Christ Jesus our Lord.

Romans 8:31-39

Paul says, "Will God ever bring an accusation against you? No! He is the one who justifies you. Will Christ (the One who died, was raised to life, and intercedes for you) condemn you? Absolutely not! He is the one who is our vindication, our guarantee." Praise God! Because of this, we have confidence before God. We know that we have been given the freedom to approach God without guilt, condemnation, or shame. We know that He will be faithful to His Word. We know that God will hear us every time we pray. And we know that His purposes, plans, and intents toward us will always be good.

Therefore, brethren, since we have full freedom and confidence to enter into the [Holy of] Holies [by the power and virtue] in the blood of Jesus, 20By this fresh (new) and living way which He initiated and dedicated and opened for us through the separating curtain (veil of the Holy of Holies), that is, through His flesh, 21And since we have [such] a great and wonderful and noble Priest [Who rules] over the house of God, 22Let us all come forward and draw near with true (honest and sincere) hearts in unqualified assurance and absolute conviction engendered by faith (by that leaning of the entire human personality on God in absolute trust and confidence in His power, wisdom, and goodness), having our hearts sprinkled and purified from a guilty (evil) conscience and our bodies cleansed with pure water. 23So let us seize and hold fast and retain without wavering the hope we cherish and confess and our acknowledgement of it, for He Who promised is reliable (sure) and faithful to His word.

Hebrews 10:19-23

For example, several years ago, I was scheduled to teach at a bible college in Atlanta. After flying in from South Africa, a representative of the school picked me up at the airport and took me to my hotel room. I was very tired. The next morning, he came to pick me up early so we could make it through traffic and get to school on time. I was still feeling a little jetlagged, but noticed a Starbucks about a block away from the hotel. Apparently, everyone in the city was tired that morning because the line was horrific. The drive-through went around the building, out of the parking lot, and into the street! I knew it wasn't possible to get through Starbucks and manage traffic that morning, so I asked if we could stop by after school. He agreed. Then I remembered my gold Starbucks card was low on cash...

Once we arrived at the school, I got busy unloading product and setting up my table. Soon a student approached me and handed me a little plastic card with a green lady on it. He said, "On my way home from work yesterday, I felt the Lord nudge me to buy you a Starbucks card. So I'd like to give you this $50 gift card."

"Wow, brother. Thanks!" I replied before turning to the man who picked me up that morning. "Look at this," I said. "God knows!"

Just before class, I walked into the auditorium and was stopped by a lady sitting on my right. She jumped up, introduced herself, and said, "Arthur, I'm pregnant."

What's that got to do with me? I thought before congratulating her. "I'm sorry," she said, "that came out wrong. What I meant was I'm a coffee drinker. I love coffee. But now that I'm pregnant, it makes me feel sick. I heard you were a coffee drinker, and I thought you might be able to use this." Then she reached into her handbag and handed me a Starbucks gift card. "I think it has around $20 left on it," she continued, "and I'd like you to have it."

I thanked her and continued to the front to put my Bible and notes on the lectern. A gentlemen a few rows back got up, walked over, and in his humble way introduced himself. "I'm from Kenya," he said. "I've lived in this country for several years, but I heard you were also from Africa."

"I'm from South Africa," I responded.

"This far from home, you almost feel like my neighbor. Anyway, last night I was heading home from the airport (that's where I work) and felt impressed to get you something. I picked up this Starbucks card. I hope you enjoy it."

Needless to say, I felt slightly overwhelmed by God's goodness that day. As a matter of fact, I continue to feel that way. I can't remember the last time I paid for a cup of Starbucks! Nearly everywhere I go, someone approaches me and gives me a Starbucks card. Sometimes it's five dollars, sometimes more, but it's always a demonstration of God's love to me. I asked the Lord about it once. He said, "Arthur, if you understood how much I love you, you would always maintain this confident expectation of good. I love you so much, I'll even support your habit!"

A while back, a man got upset with me for telling that story. He said, "How can you tell such a frivolous story? Some people have legitimate needs they're believing God for."

I replied, "Brother, that story should give you hope. It should encourage you. If our Father would look at something so miniscule as my preference for a cup of coffee from Starbucks and work behind the scenes everywhere I go to bless me with it, how much more will He supply the needs in your life? That's what hope is—a confident expectation of good. I have an expectation now that I will never have to pay for a cup of Starbucks, and God meets that expectation. He fulfills my hopes."

And this hope will not lead to disappointment. For we know how dearly God loves us...

Romans 5:5 (NLT)

I hope that story encourages you. Over the years, I've discovered that if we don't feel we can "bother" God with the small things, then we'll not bother Him with anything. If we can't trust Him in the small things, how can we trust Him in the big things? (Matt. 6:25-34) But when we come to understand what God has done for us, we will have confidence before Him. We will know His character and expect Him to perform His word in our lives. We will remember that Jesus' work has become our reward!

If we can't trust Him in the small things, how can we trust Him in the big things?

Bless (affectionately, gratefully praise) the Lord, O my soul; and all that is [deepest] within me, bless His holy name! ²Bless (affectionately, gratefully praise) the Lord, O my soul, and forget not [one of] all His benefits—3Who forgives [every one of] all your iniquities, Who heals [each one of] all your diseases, 4Who redeems your life from the pit and corruption, Who beautifies, dignifies, and crowns you with loving-kindness and tender mercy; 5Who satisfies your mouth [your necessity and desire at your personal age and situation] with good so that your youth, renewed, is like the eagle's [strong, overcoming, soaring]!... ¹⁰He has not dealt with us after our sins nor rewarded us according to our iniquities. ¹¹For as the heavens are high above the earth, so great are His mercy and loving-kindness toward those who reverently and worshipfully fear Him. [12]As far as the east is from the west, so far has He removed our transgressions from us. [13]As a father loves and pities his children, so the Lord loves and pities those who fear Him [with reverence, worship, and awe].

Psalm 103:1–5, 10–13

Chapter Seven

THE RESPONSE OF RELATIONSHIP

Legalism—the opposite of new covenant relationship—is anything we think we have to do, ought to do, or shouldn't do in order to keep God happy, to stay in His favor, and to receive what He has freely given us in Christ. Legalism creates bondage and ultimately leads to lip service (Isa. 29:13). Any amount of legalism in our belief system produces feelings of guilt and obligation that say, "I owe God this service." Obligation speaks to indebtedness, but the "debt" we owed God could never be repaid by us. That's why Jesus came.

Jesus unequivocally displayed God's grace to us. But did you know that grace has always been part of God's nature? (Heb. 13:8, James 1:17, and Ps. 89:34) In Exodus when Moses asked God to show him His glory, God said, "I will proclaim My Name to you, and I will be gracious to whom I will be gracious." (Ex. 33:19) And later when

God passed by, He said of Himself, I am "Yahweh, the God who is merciful and gracious, slow to anger, and abounding in steadfast love and faithfulness." (Ex. 34:6) Even in the Old Covenant, God tied His Name to grace, love, and faithfulness and announced to Moses that He would "decide to whom to show my grace." Brothers and sisters, God has explicitly shown His grace to us in the person of Jesus Christ! Jesus' finished work so completely destroyed performance-based relationship that there can be no more argument about God's character, His love for us, or what is necessary to please Him. The only question that remains is, "What will our response be?"

> *Jesus came and opened the way to relationship with God for us, regardless of our performance or worthiness.*

The reality of the Gospel is grace. Jesus came and opened the way to relationship with God for us, regardless of our performance or worthiness. He came to demonstrate what had been in God's heart all along:

This is how much God loved the world: He gave his Son, his one and only Son. And this is why: so that no one need be destroyed; by believing in him, anyone can have a whole and lasting life. God didn't go to all the trouble of sending his Son merely to point an accusing finger, telling the world how bad it was. He came to help, to put the world right again. Anyone who trusts in him is acquitted; anyone who refuses to trust him has long since been under the death sentence without knowing it. And why? Because of

that person's failure to believe in the one-of-a-kind
Son of God when introduced to him.

John 3:16-18 (MSG)

By this the love of God was manifested in us, that
God has sent His only begotten Son into the world so
that we might live through Him. 10In this is love,
not that we loved God, but that He loved us and sent
His Son to be the propitiation for our sins.

1 John 4:9-10 (NASB)

Man, what a statement! It wasn't our great desire to
have relationship with God (remember our guilt kept us
from that) that eventually won God over and exposed His
love for us. It was His love for us that said, "I'm willing to
do whatever it takes to bring My beloved children back
to intimate relationship with Me." Now all we have to do
to receive that love is repent and believe.

Jesus told them, "This is the only work God wants
from you: Believe in the one he has sent."

John 6:29 (NLT)

Remember, therefore, what you have received and
heard; hold it fast, and repent...

Revelation 3:3a (NIV)

So repent (change your mind and purpose); turn
around and return [to God], that your sins may
be erased (blotted out, wiped clean), that times of
refreshing (of recovering from the effects of heat, of
reviving with fresh air) may come from the presence
of the Lord.

Acts 3:19

The word *"repent"* is often misunderstood. It is often
touted as the *"feeling and expression of sincere regret."*

(Dictionary.com) But that definition is not biblical. "Repent" is the Greek word *metanoeo*, which literally means, "to change one's thinking; to reconsider." (Thayer, 2002) Repenting is the process of renewing our minds (Eph. 4:23). It includes changing our thoughts and opinions, reevaluating our perception, and conforming our belief system to God's (Rom. 12:2). Repenting is what Jesus said our response to the demonstration of God's grace should be.

However, if we refuse to repent and accept God's free gift of grace, instead rejecting the finished work of Christ, "there remains no more sacrifice for sin." (Heb. 10:26) Let me explain what that means. Jesus said, "I am the way, the truth, and the life. No one comes to the Father except through me." (John 14:6) Apart from Jesus, there is no other way to atone for sin; there is no other way to be saved or experience God's kind of life. There is no other way to reach heaven. If we reject the Way to relationship God has offered, there isn't another.

> *For if we sin willfully after we have received the knowledge of the truth, there remains no more sacrifice for sins.*
>
> *Hebrews 10:26 (KJV 2000)*

Now let me explain what this is **not** saying. This is not saying that if you mess up after receiving Christ, there is no other sacrifice for your sin. The Living Bible translates this verse as "If anyone sins deliberately by rejecting the Savior after knowing the truth of forgiveness, this sin is not covered by Christ's death; there is no way to get rid of it." So if someone hears the complete and true message of reconciliation—the message of grace— yet willfully rejects Christ saying, "I don't need Your payment," that person has no other recourse—no other way of atonement, except the one offered in and through the blood of Jesus Christ. There remains no other way to Life in God!

But repenting is not just something we do to "be saved." Repenting is conforming our belief system to God's, and for many of us, it is a life-long process. Perhaps you no longer need to repent of going your own way and rejecting Christ's sacrifice, but you may need to repent like Job and say, "Surely I spoke of things I did not understand...My ears had heard of You, but now my eyes have seen You...I repent." (Job 42:3, 5-6 NIV) Perhaps you have areas of belief or ways of thinking that do not match God's. Perhaps that is your needed response. You see, our response is what positions us to receive the benefits of our relationship with God.

> **Repenting is conforming our belief system to God's, and for many of us, it is a life-long process.**

Years ago, I needed to repent to position myself to receive the blessings God had for me. I wasn't "living in sin," but I had not completely renewed my mind with the truth of God's love. I still struggled to see myself as God did and hadn't grasped the fullness of the meaning of my adoption into sonship. I hadn't understood the verse in Romans that says, "The Spirit himself testifies with our spirit that we are God's children. Now if we are children, then we are heirs—heirs of God and co-heirs with Christ, if indeed we share in his sufferings in order that we may also share in his glory." (Rom. 8:16-17) Then the Lord spoke to me and said, "Arthur, if you can discover how much I love you, you will never ask me for another cent. The moment you understand how much I love you, you will know your needs are met." God's statement rocked my world, and I immediately repented and began to change my thinking process to line up with His Word.

Not Lip Service, Heart Service

This is the agreement (testament, covenant) that I will set up and conclude with them after those days, says the Lord: I will imprint My laws upon their hearts, and I will inscribe them on their minds (on their inmost thoughts and understanding).
Hebrews 10:16

With God's law written on our hearts, our service (response) to Him should also come from our hearts. But what law is it that God writes on our hearts? The law of liberty (James 1:25, 2:12, and John 8:32). In Paul's letter to the Galatians, we find this law explained. In it he says, "It is for liberty wherewith Christ has made us free." (Gal. 5:1) Liberty is "the freedom from control, interference, obligation, restriction, or hampering conditions; it is the power or right of doing, thinking, and speaking according to one's own choice." (Dictionary.com) So if Christ set us free for freedom's sake, then our service to God should be without obligation. We should not serve God because we feel we owe Him something. Our response should be one of gratitude and love that flows from our innermost being. That is the type of relationship God desires; and that is the type of relationship He designed us for.

But the hour cometh, and now is, when the true worshippers shall worship the Father in spirit and in truth: for the Father seeketh such to worship him. ²⁴God is a Spirit: and they that worship him must worship him in spirit and in truth.

John 4:23-24 (KJV)

This subtle change in our response is what changes our "lip service" to an act of worship and intimate relationship with God (Mark 7:6-7). It will cause us to start living better by accident than we ever did on purpose and fuel our transition into guilt-free living. John said:

Dear children, let us not love in words only nor with the lips, but in deed and in truth. ¹⁹And in this way we shall come to know that we are loyal to the truth, and shall satisfy our consciences in His presence ²⁰in whatever matters our hearts condemn us— because God is greater than our hearts and knows everything.

1 John 3:18-20 (WNT)

Living from our hearts—our deepest subconscious beliefs and persuasions—is how we live guilt-free. As Christians, our hearts should be the driving force of our lives and decision-making. Romans says, "For those who are according to the flesh set their minds on the things of the flesh, but those who are according to the Spirit, the things of the Spirit. For the mind set on the flesh is death, but the mind set on the Spirit is life and peace." (Rom. 8:5-

As Christians, our hearts should be the driving force of our lives and decision-making.

6 NIV) Heart living is supernatural living. It is doing the things that lead to life and peace that we want to do, not the things we have to do. But even if we mess up, John says, "God is greater than our hearts." His plans for us and good intentions toward us will not change; Christ's sacrifice is still enough. And if we accidently start living better out of our hearts than we did out of all our self-effort and guilt, we have "perfect confidence towards God."

> *Dear friends, if our hearts do not condemn us, we have perfect confidence towards God; *[22]*and whatever we ask for we obtain from Him, because we obey His commands and do the things which are pleasing in His sight. *[23]*And this is His command—that we are to believe in His Son Jesus Christ and love one another, just as He has commanded us to do. *[24]*The man who obeys His commands continues in union with God, and God continues in union with him; and through His Spirit whom He has given us we can know that He continues in union with us.*
>
> *1 John 3: 21-24 (WNT)*

You see, when we recognize and begin renewing our minds to all that Christ accomplished for us, Paul says the love of Christ is what constrains us. It is His work in our hearts that becomes the ruling factor for what we believe, do, and say.

> *For the love of Christ constrains us; because we thus judge, that if one died for all, then were all dead: And that he died for all, that they who live should no longer live unto themselves, but unto him who died for them, and rose again.*
>
> *2 Corinthians 5:14 (KJV 2000)*

This "constraint" doesn't happen because He forces it on us or because we know it's the right thing to do and force it ourselves. It happens as a natural outflow of His love. When Paul says, "the love of Christ constrains us," he means that God's love lays siege on our hearts. When an army lays siege on a city, it encompasses and surrounds the city to become the dominating factor of what goes into and out of that city. When we understand the Gospel—the love of Christ and what He accomplished for us—that knowledge becomes the dominating force of what we allow to come into and go out of our hearts. Why? Because according to Galatians, we are dead, "I am crucified with Christ: nevertheless I live; yet not I, but Christ liveth in me: and the life which I now live in the flesh I live by the faith of the Son of God, who loved me, and gave himself for me." (Gal. 2:20 KJV) We died in Christ and no longer live life unto ourselves but unto Him, or we could say, because Christ died as me, I now live as Him.

We always carry around in our body the death of Jesus, so that the life of Jesus may also be revealed in our body.
2 Corinthians 4:10 NIV

That's what the message of grace is all about. It's not something to be squandered and used as an excuse to live however we want; it's the power of God to live life as His children and experience the benefits of relationship with Him, including the freedom from guilt, shame, and condemnation. Because of this, Paul continues:

Consequently, from now on we estimate and regard no one from a [purely] human point of view [in terms of natural standards of value]. [No] even though we

*once did estimate Christ from a human viewpoint
and as a man, yet now [we have such knowledge of
Him that] we know Him no longer [in terms of the
flesh].*

2 Corinthians 5:16

The Gospel changes things. It changes what you believe about God but also what you believe about yourself. Instead of only seeing my failures and feeling unworthy of relationship with God, the Gospel teaches me to view the world (and myself) from His perspective. Not only that, but now, everywhere I go and every person I see, I can see through the eyes of Christ. I can bypass their outward appearance and external behavior and see them in a way that they might not even see themselves—as a lost but beloved child of God.

*Therefore if any person is [ingrafted] in Christ
(the Messiah) he is a new creation (a new creature
altogether); the old [previous moral and spiritual
condition] has passed away. Behold, the fresh and
new has come! ¹⁸But all things are from God, Who
through Jesus Christ reconciled us to Himself [received
us into favor, brought us into harmony with Himself]
and gave to us the ministry of reconciliation [that by
word and deed we might aim to bring others into
harmony with Him].*

2 Corinthians 5:17-18

God has done everything necessary to make relationship available to you and me—even to the point of giving up His own Son. What will your response be?

A NOTE FROM ARTHUR

I encourage you to take your time reading this book. Study the scriptures I've included, and let the Holy Spirit reveal the truth of God's Word to you. Allow the Word to renew your mind and change your opinions of God and His purposes for your life. Feed your spirit with good teaching about righteousness and the love of God. And don't forget to surround yourself with believers who will encourage you through this revelation process into guilt-free living.

If you're interested, you can review some of my study notes in the following resources:

"Alienate." Merriam-Webster.com. Merriam-Webster, n.d. Web. 22 August 2015. <http://www.merriam-webster.com/dictionary/alienate>.

Archer, Gleason, Dr. and Gary Hill. HELPS Word-studies. Chicago: Moody Publishers, 1987. Electronic database retrieved from: www.biblehub.com.

Dictionary.com Unabridged. Random House, Inc., n.d. Web. 22 August 2015. <Dictionary.com http://dictionary.reference.com/browse>.

"Facts about Niagara Falls." Niagarafallslive.com Web. 22 August 2015. <http://www.niagarafallslive.com/Facts_about_Niagara_Falls.htm>.

Hecht, Mendy. "Shabbat Q&A with Rabbi Mendy Hecht." Askmoses.com 2015. <http://www.askmoses.com/en/article/208,146/How-far-am-I-allowed-to-walk-on-Shabbat.html>.

Thayer, Joseph and James Strong. Thayer's Greek-English Lexicon of the New Testament. Biblesoft, Inc. 2002. Electronic database retrieved from: www.biblehub.com.

Please feel free to contact me if you have questions or would like someone to agree with you in prayer. I'd also love to hear your testimonies or receive your feedback from this book. You can contact me online at www.kingdomlifeministry.com. God's richest blessings are yours!

Made in the USA
Charleston, SC
13 December 2015